PATASSO

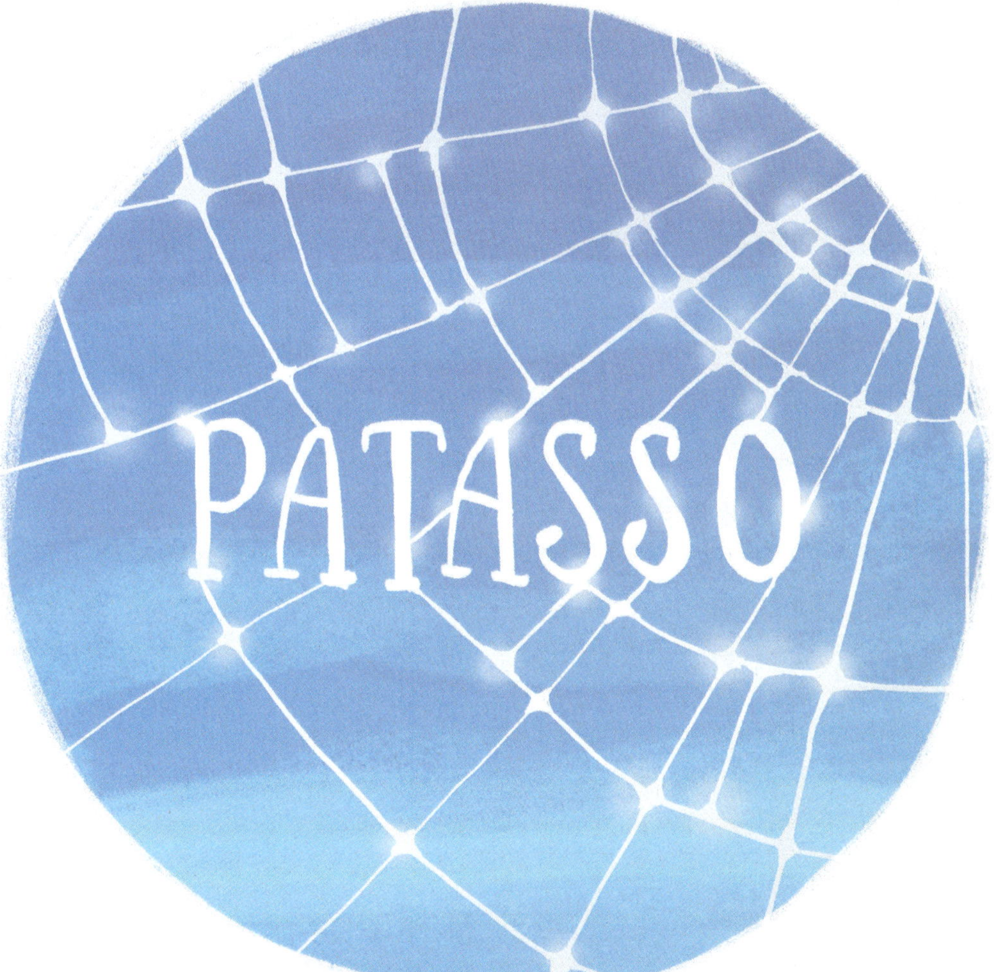

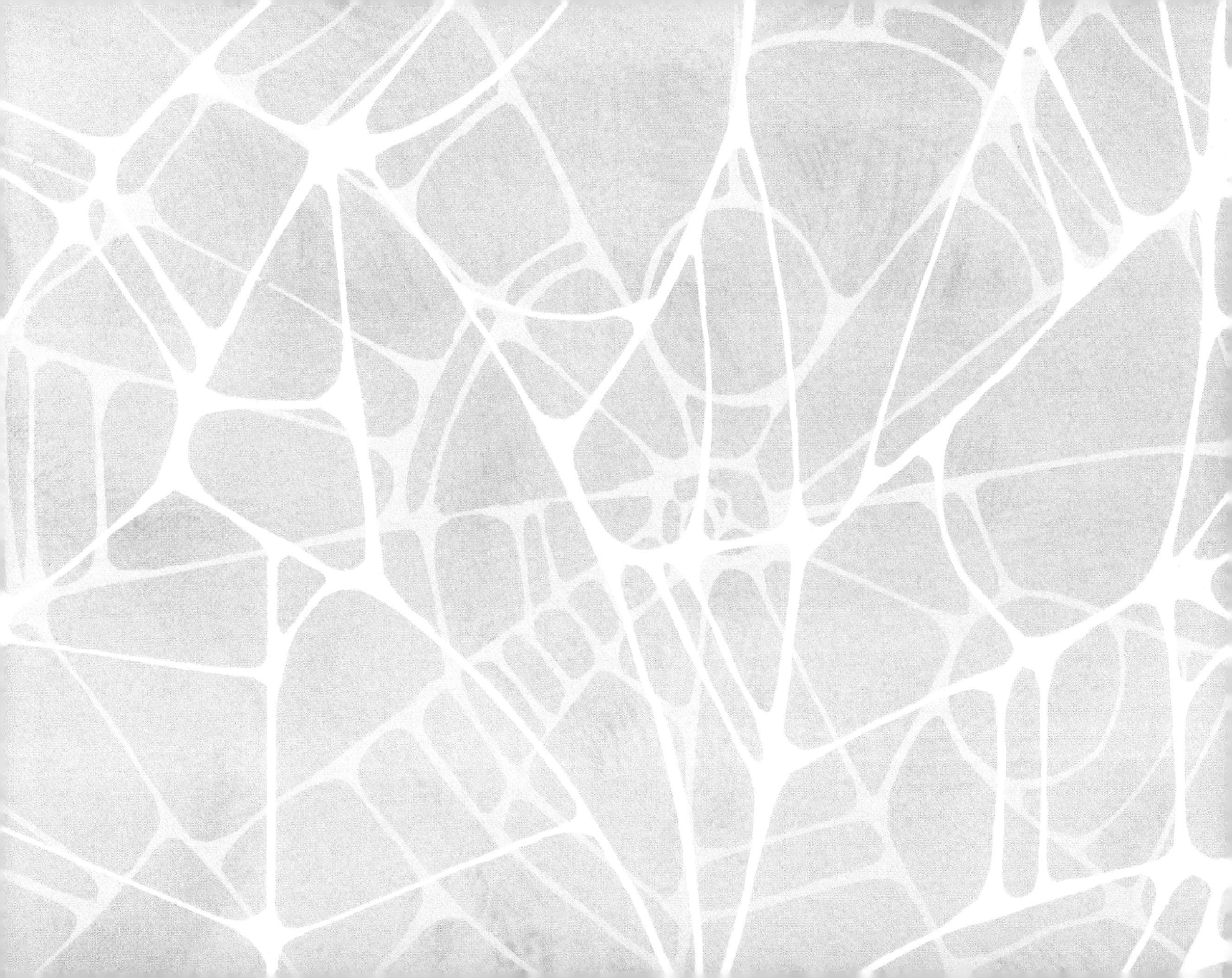

Tracy Bayley

PATASSO

Illustrated by
Julia Elaine

ISBN 978-1-66782-329-4

To my mother & father...
You've been a constant in my life. You taught me faith in God,
unconditional love and commitment to family.
Love you more!

In honor of my mother-in-law Sam,
who dreamed up the concept of Patasso
and raised an incredible man that I love.

Thank you Julia Elaine for bringing Patasso to life
with your beautiful illustrations, imagination & talent!

T. B.

To anyone who creates, keep going.

J. E.

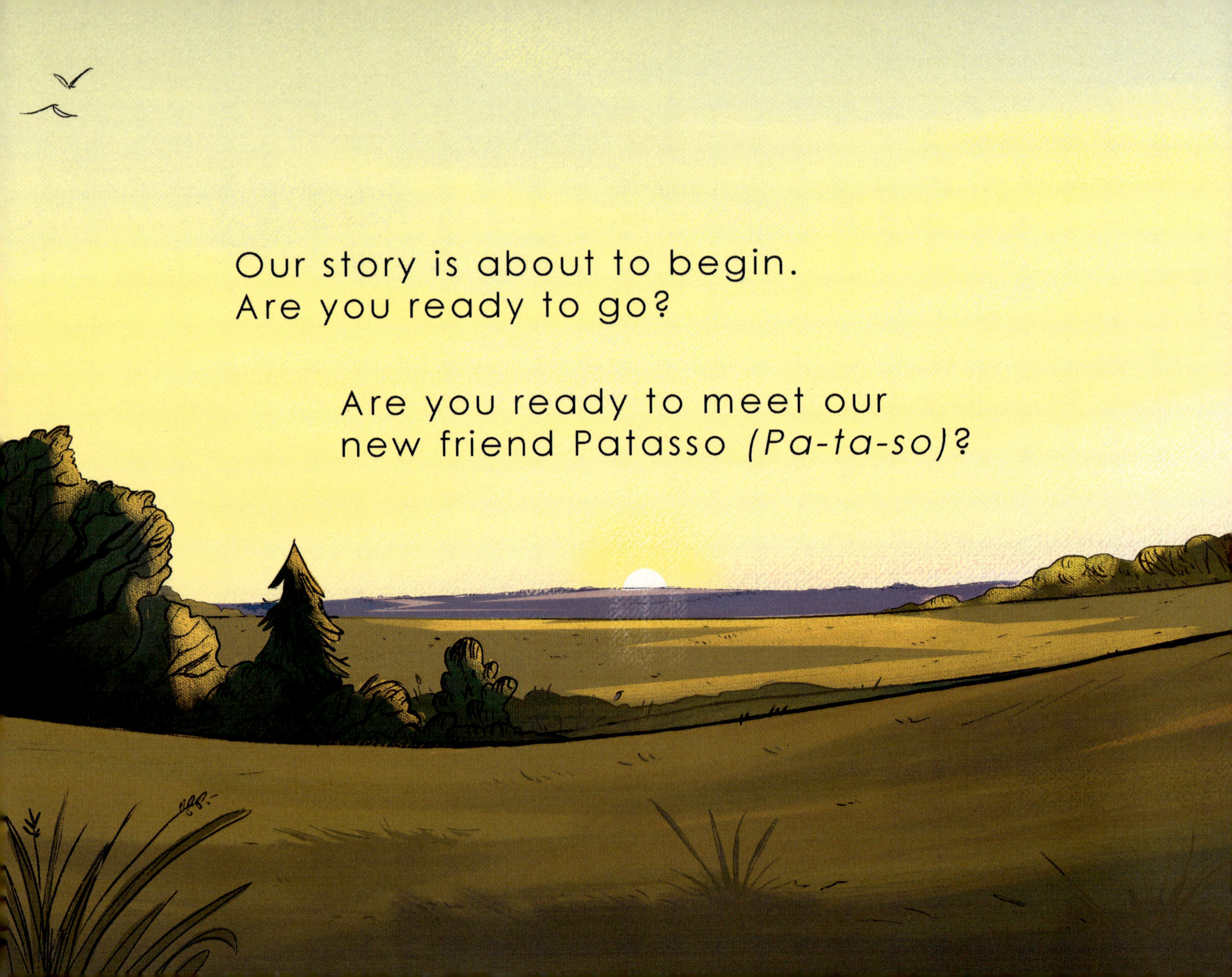
Our story is about to begin.
Are you ready to go?

Are you ready to meet our
new friend Patasso (Pa-ta-so)?

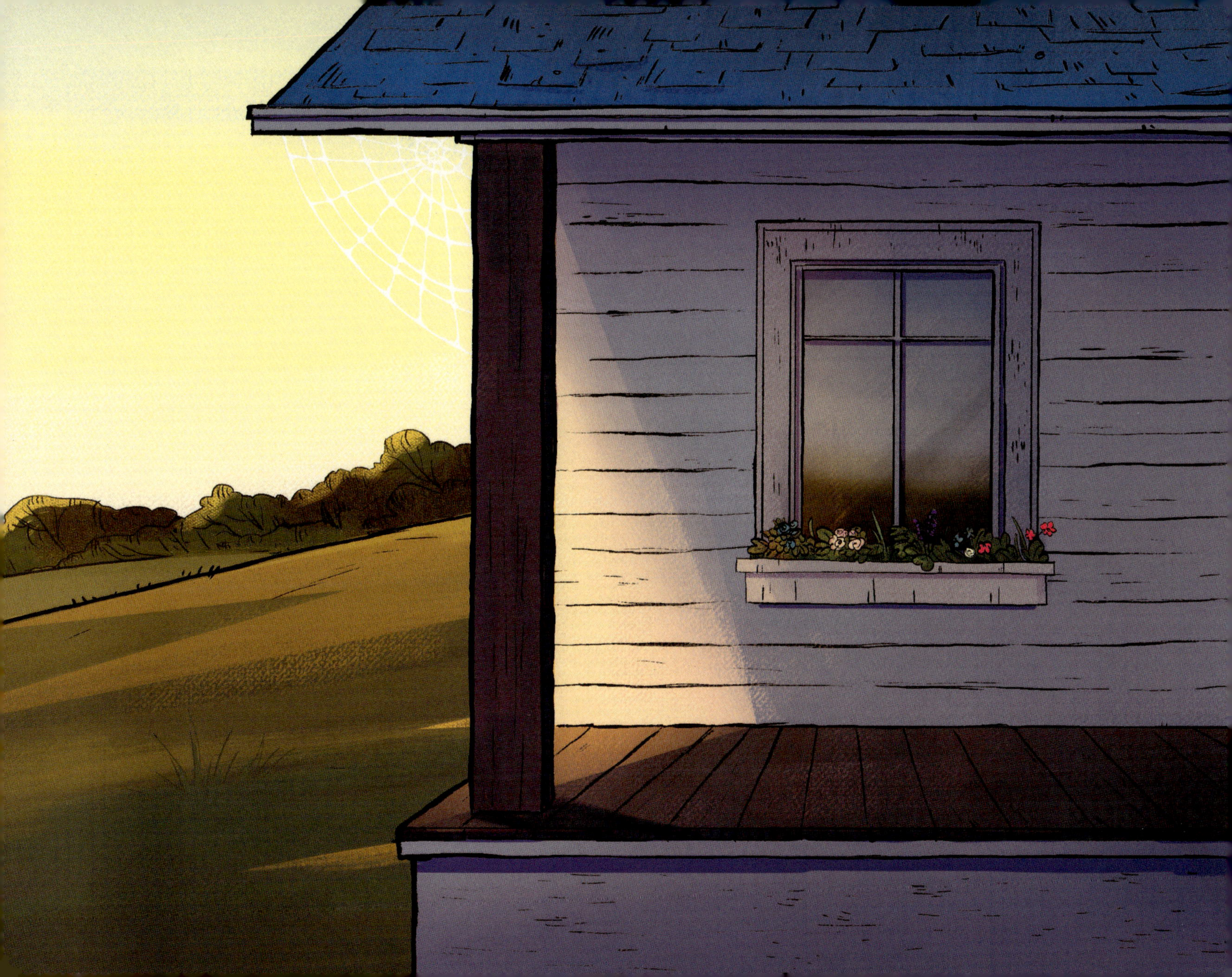

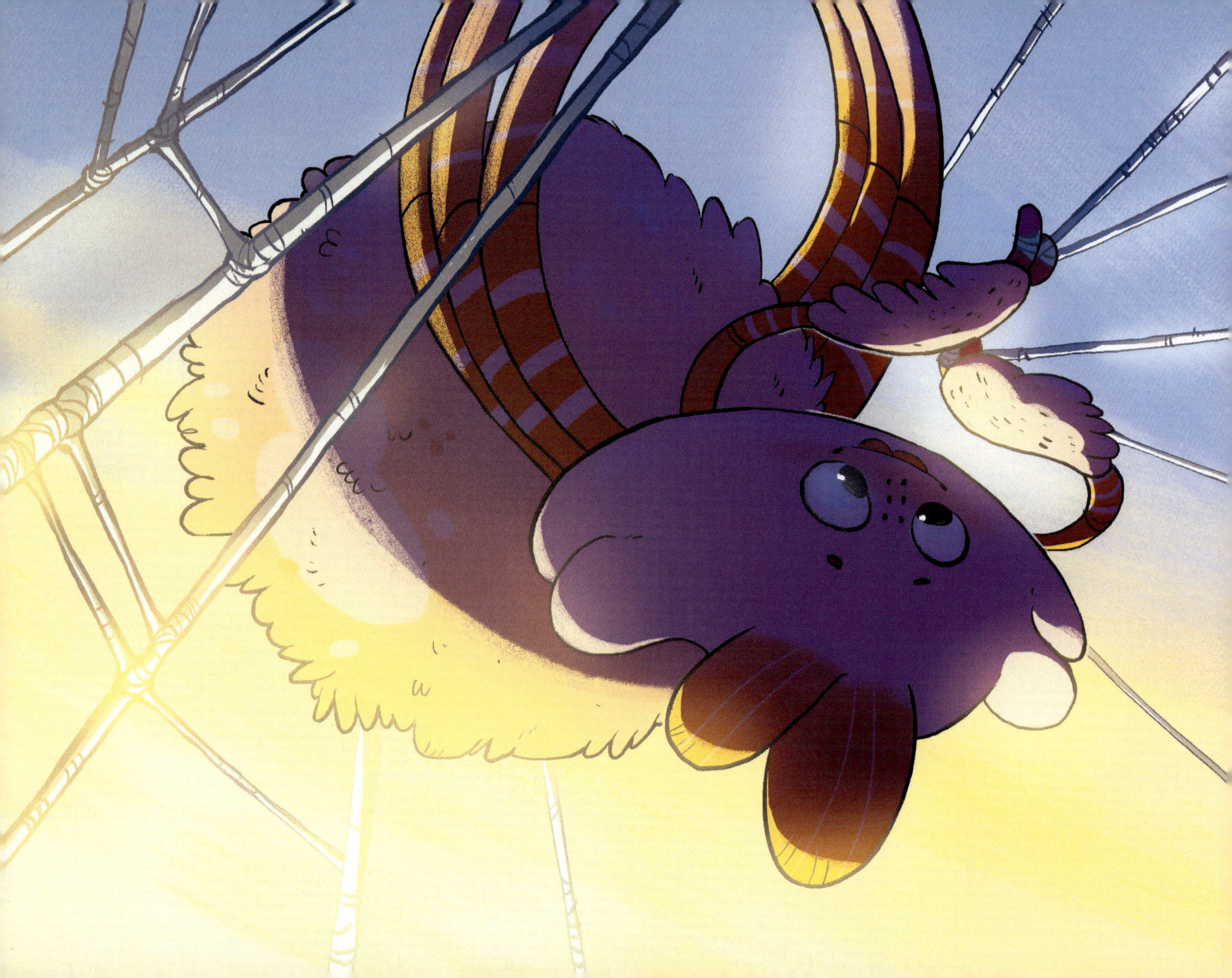

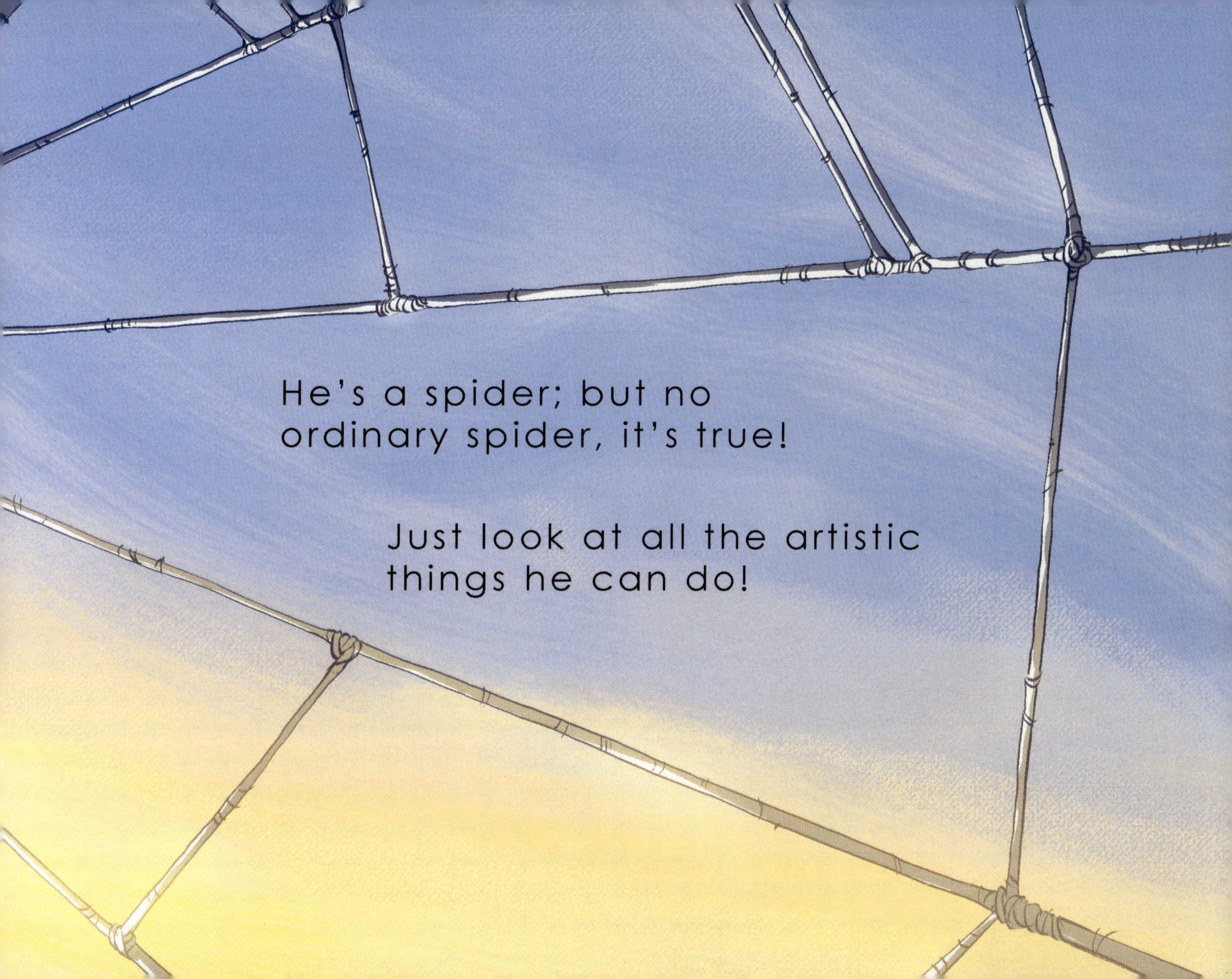
He's a spider; but no
ordinary spider, it's true!

Just look at all the artistic
things he can do!

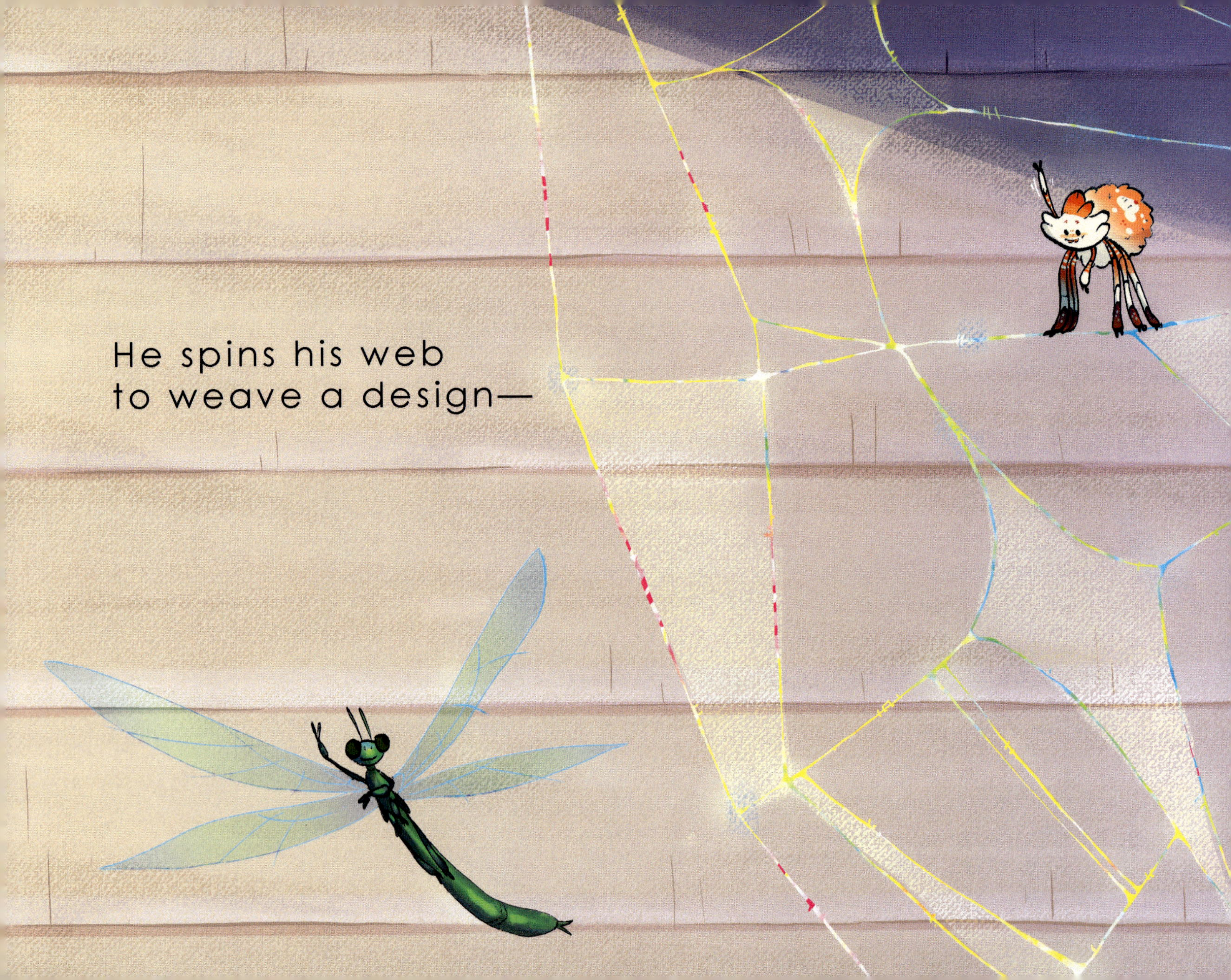
He spins his web
to weave a design—

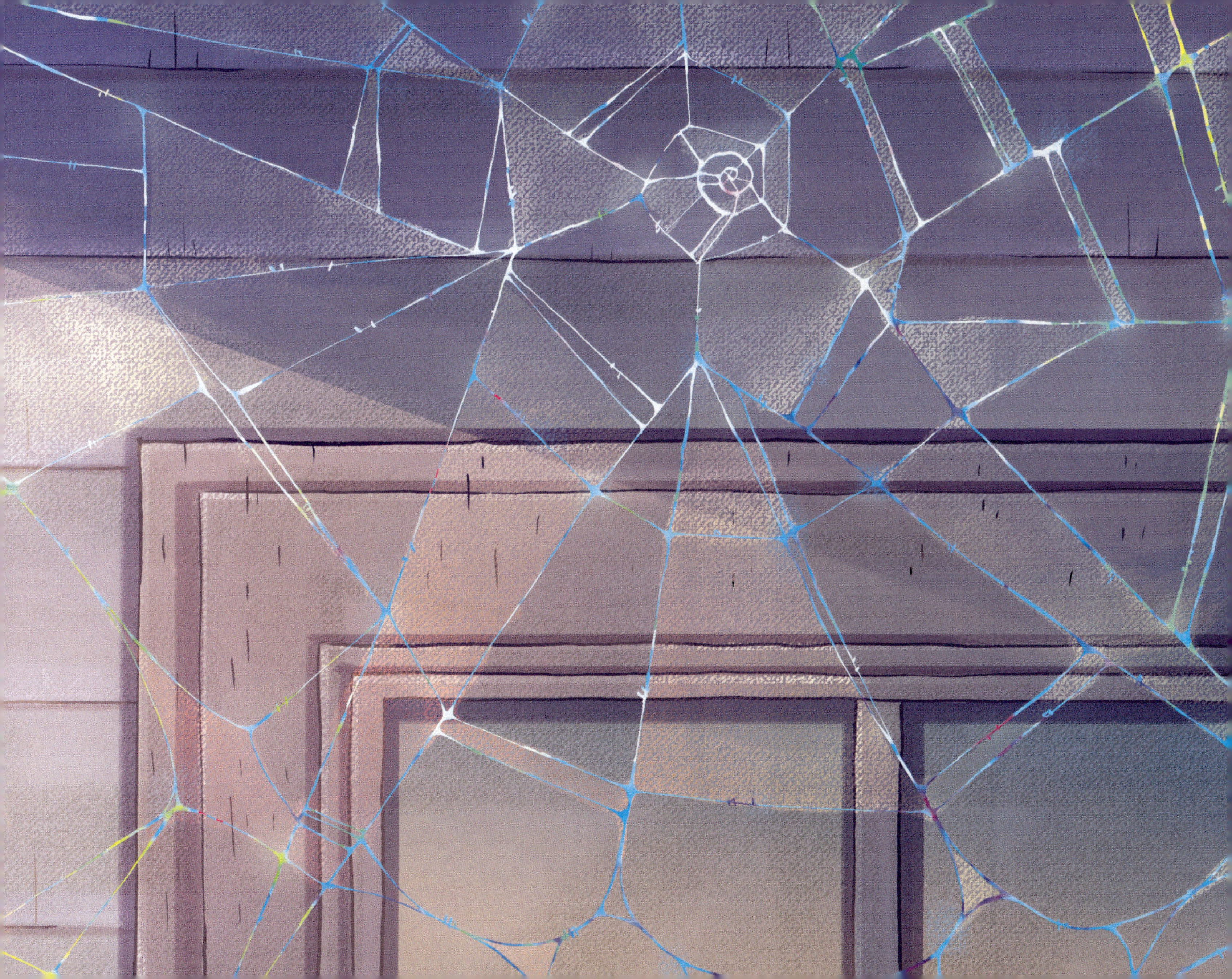

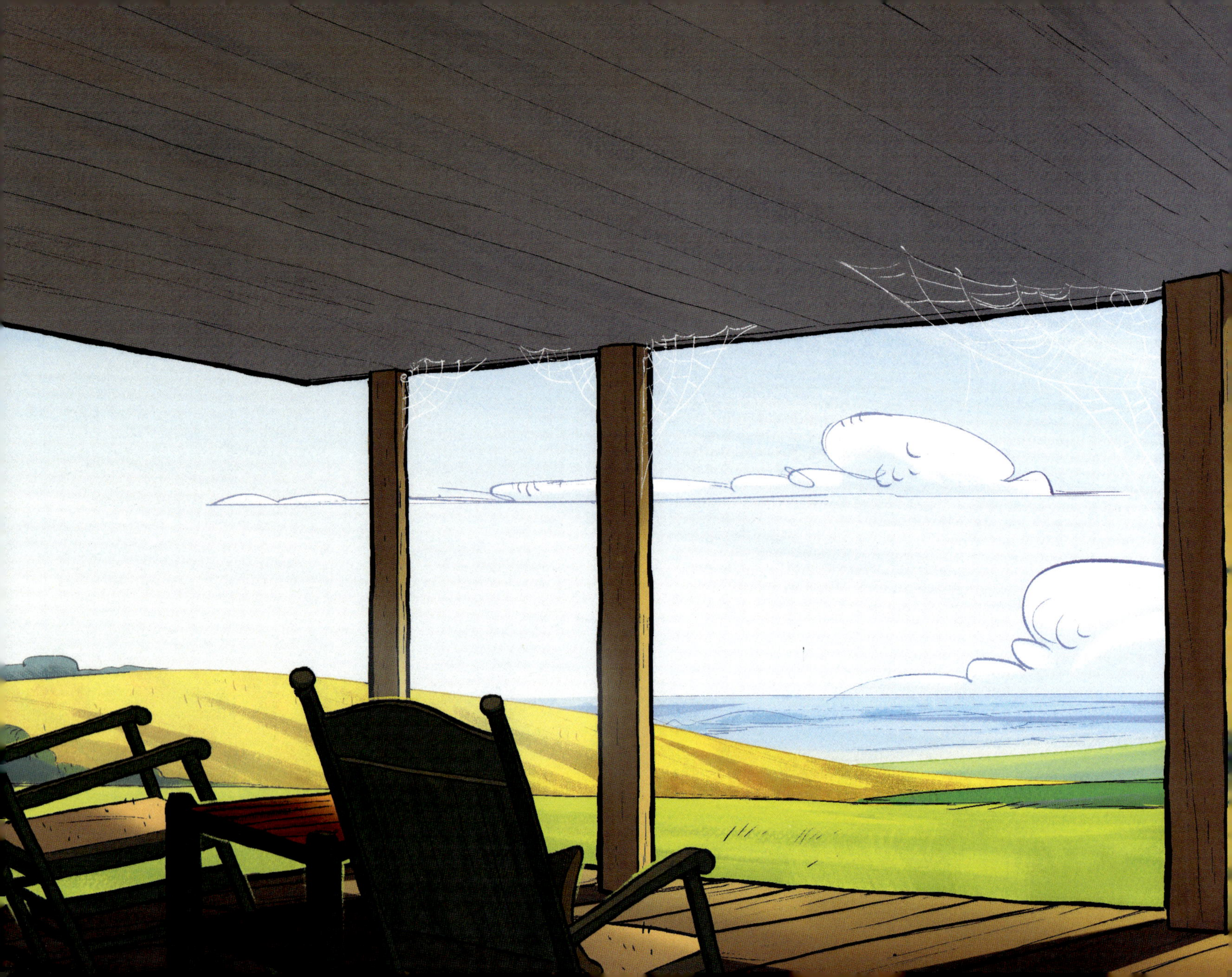

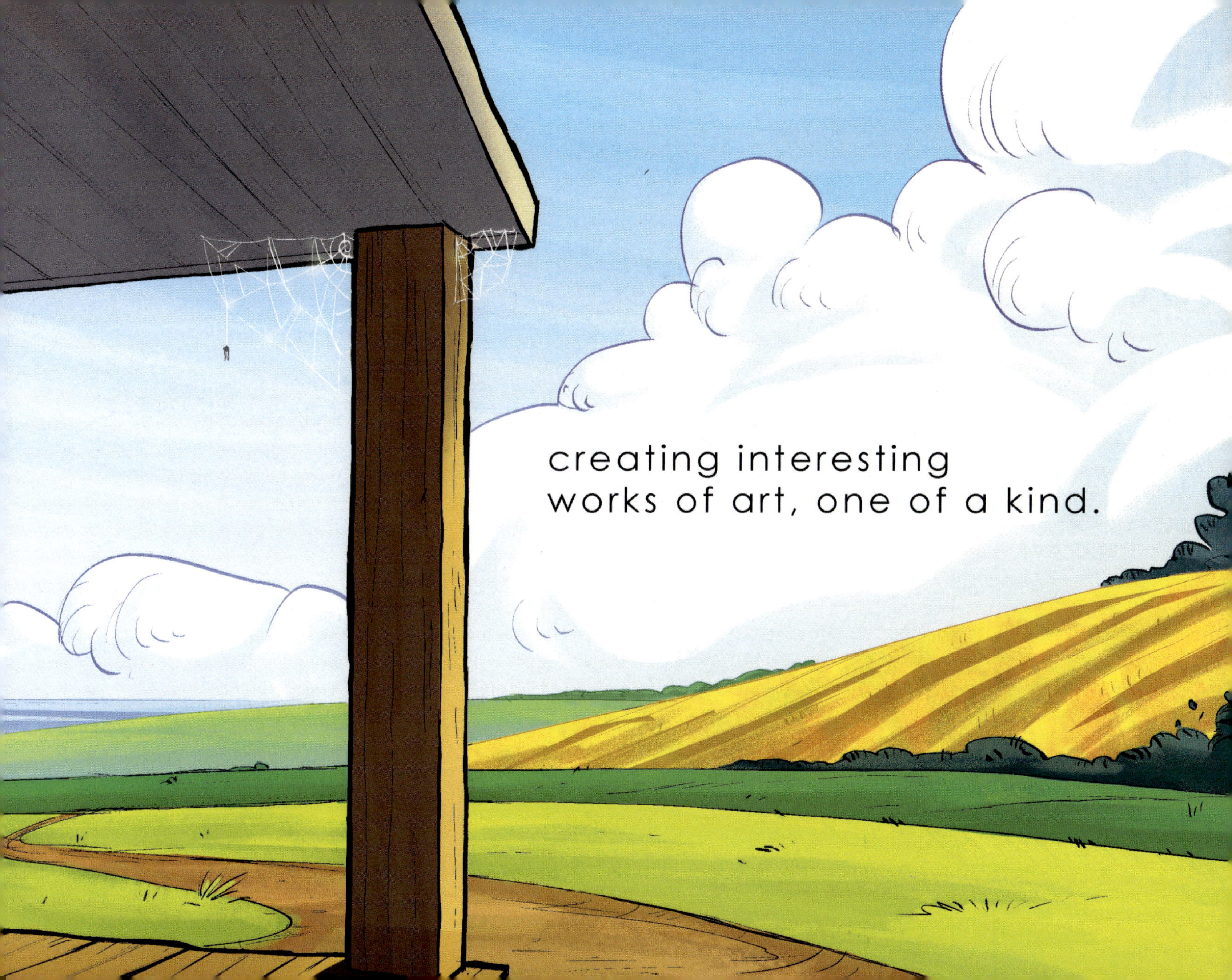

creating interesting
works of art, one of a kind.

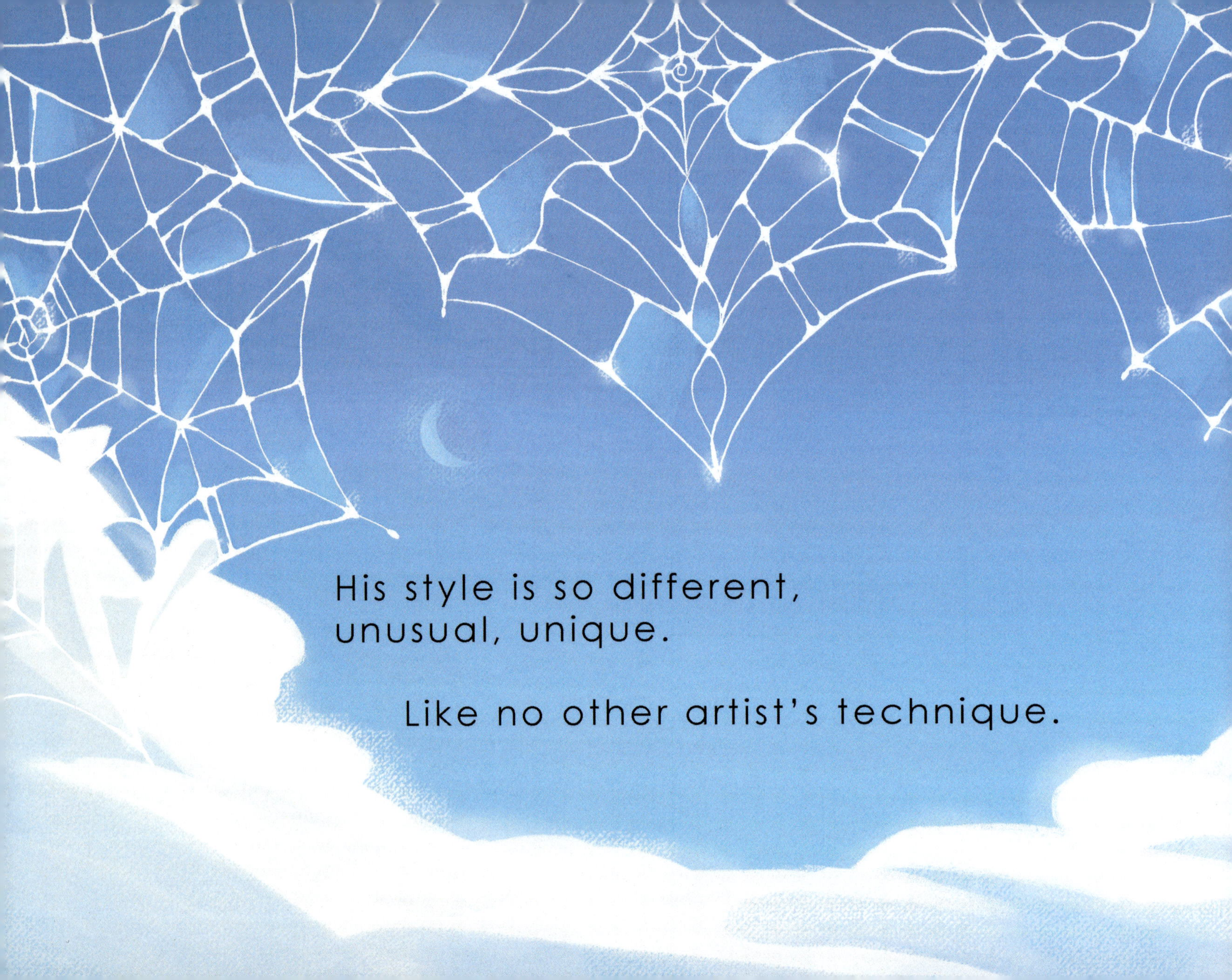
His style is so different,
unusual, unique.

Like no other artist's technique.

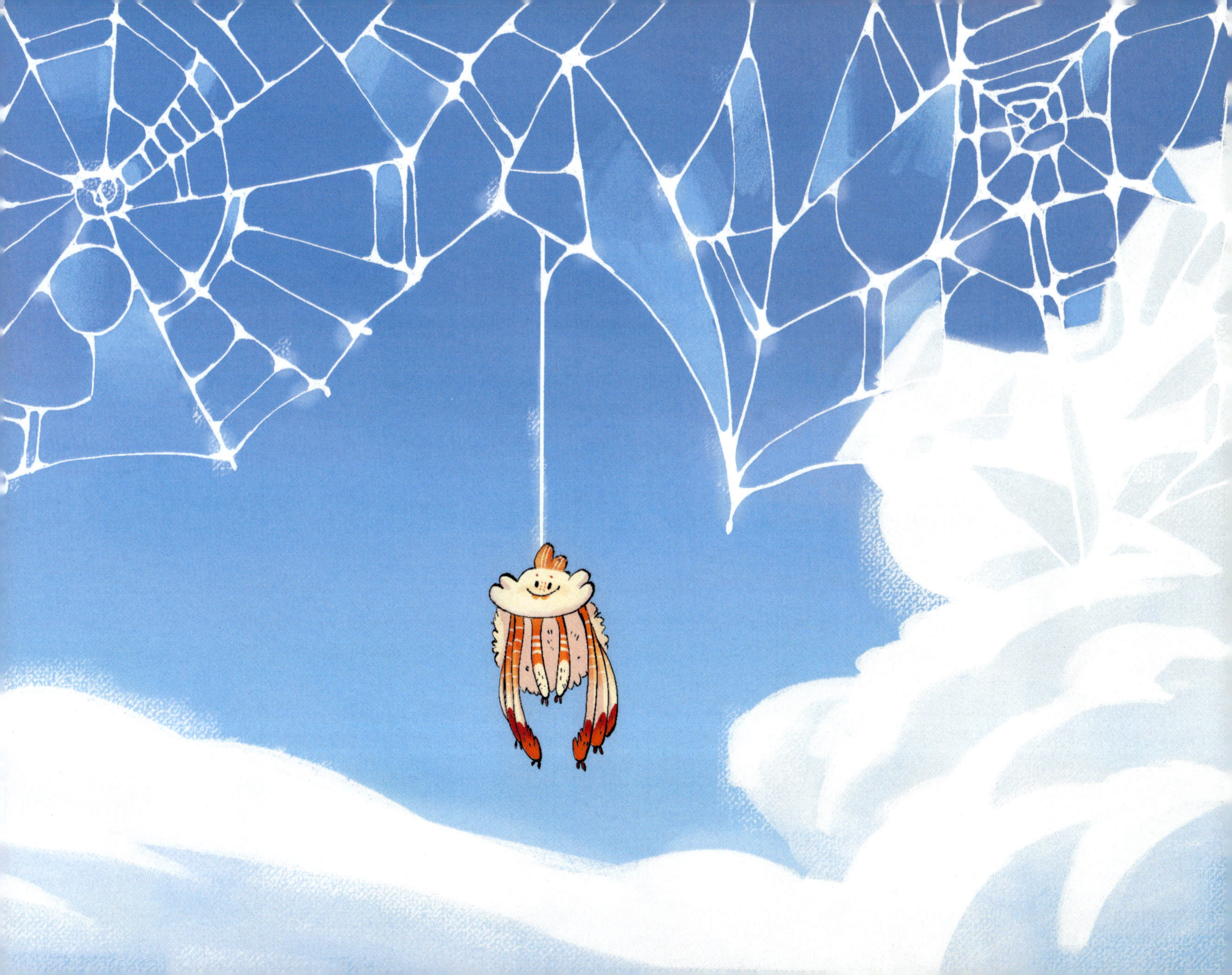

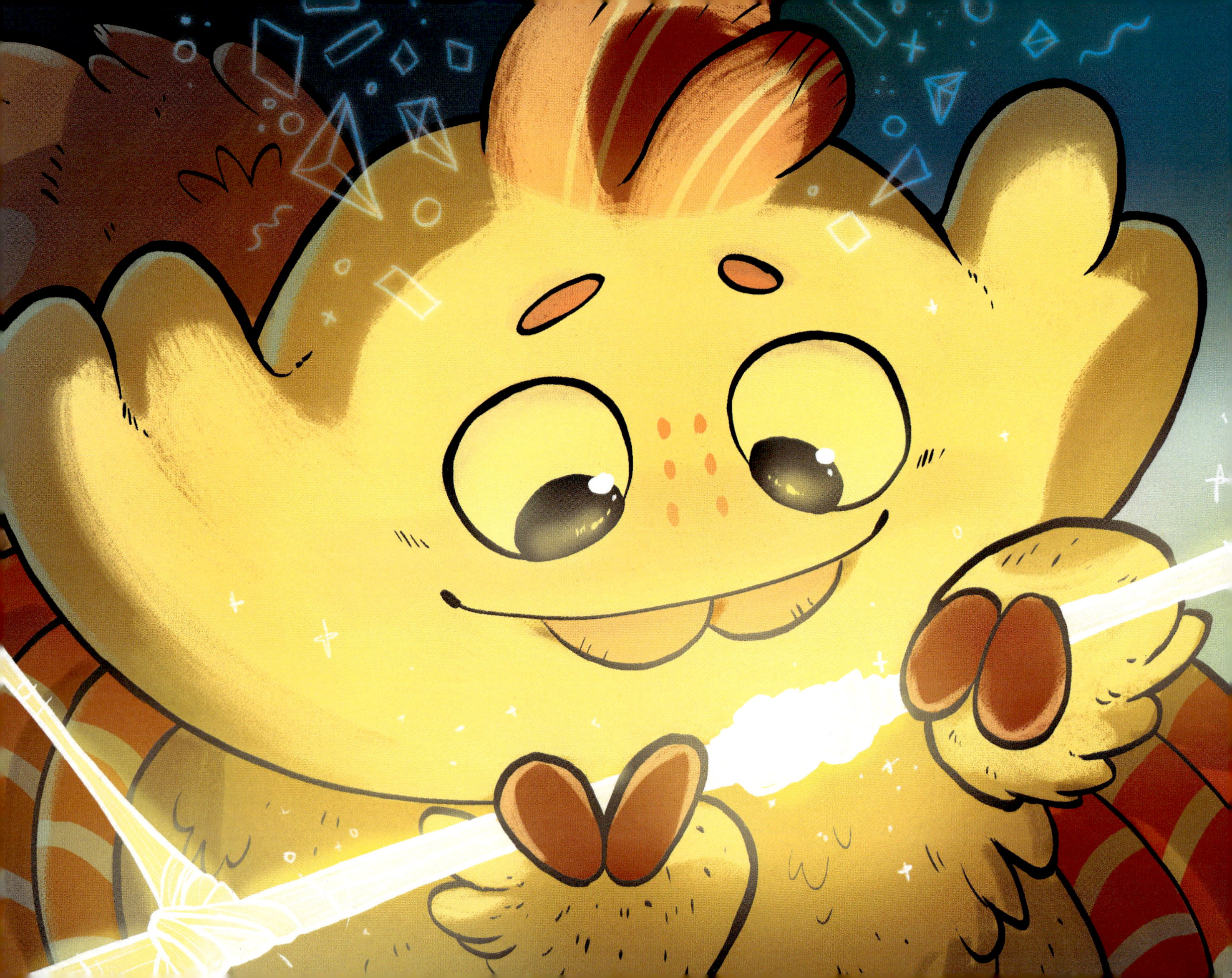

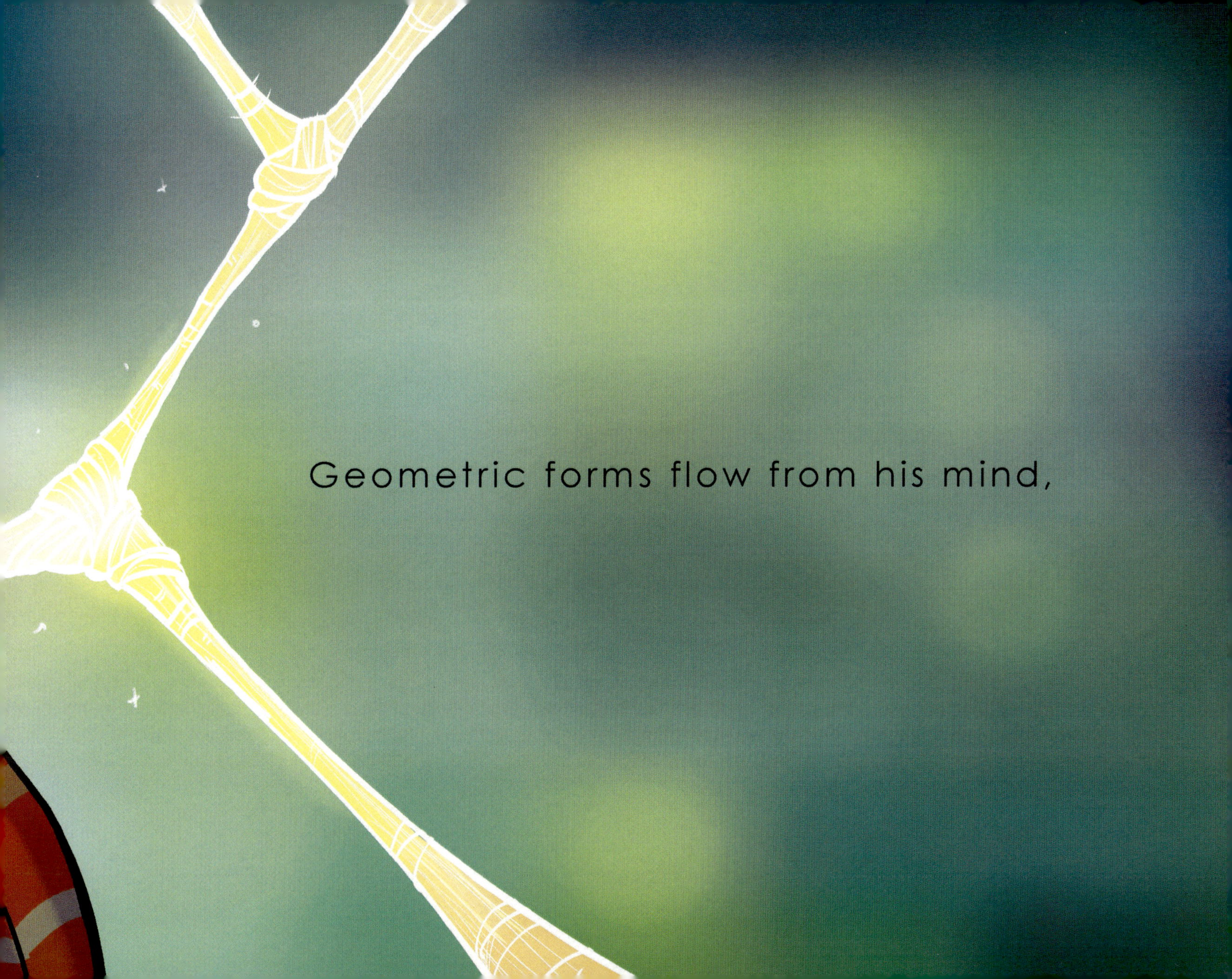

Geometric forms flow from his mind,

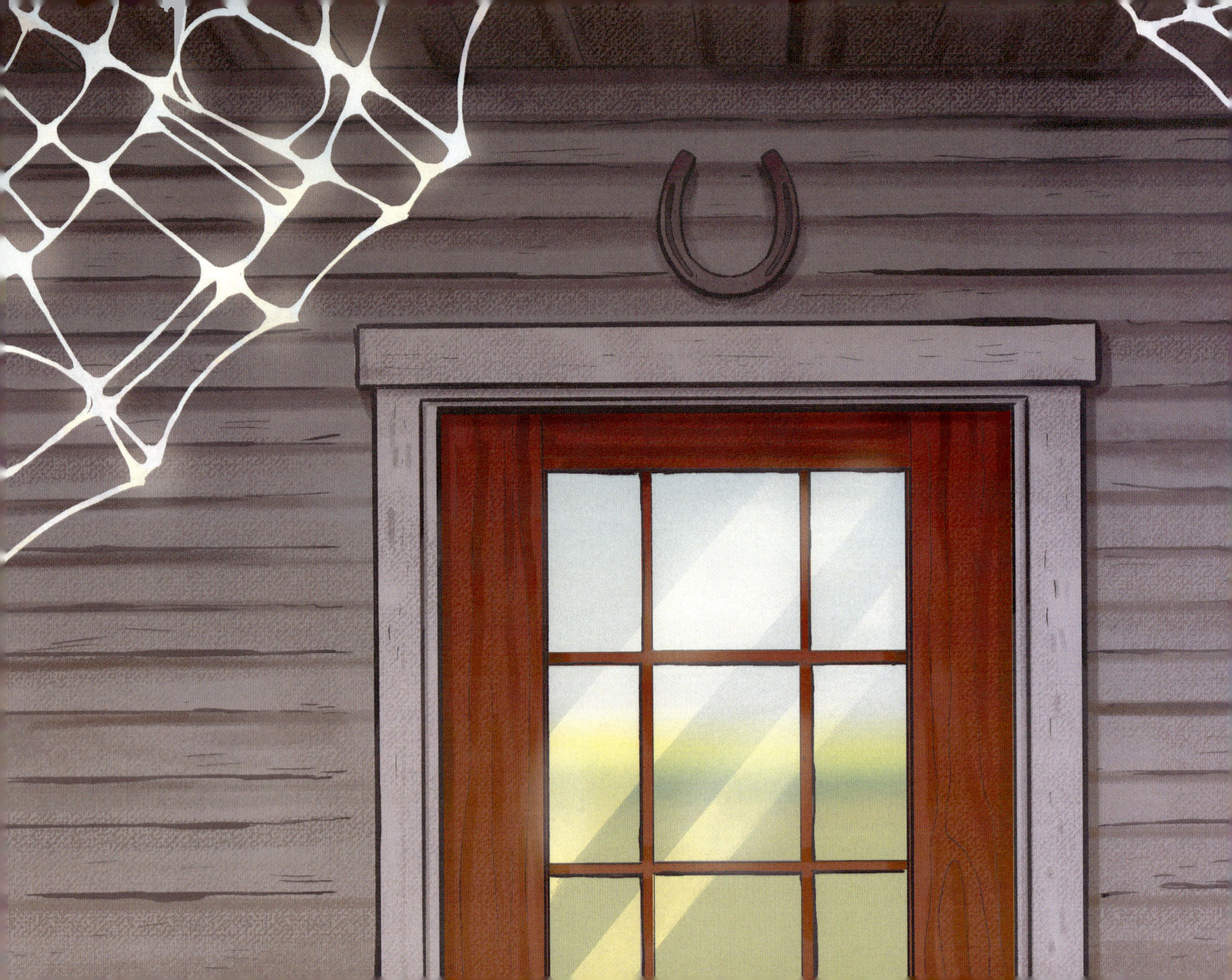

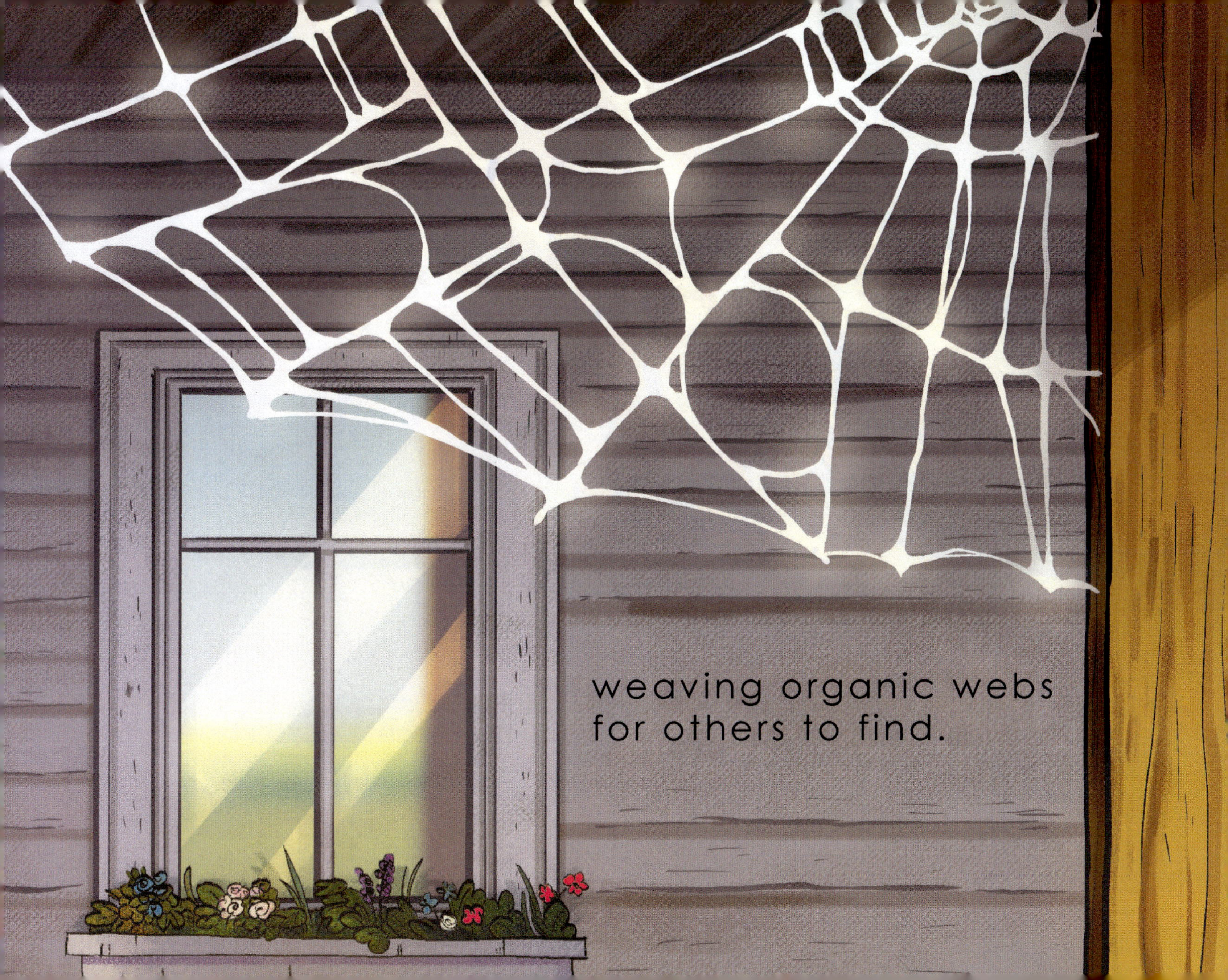
weaving organic webs
for others to find.

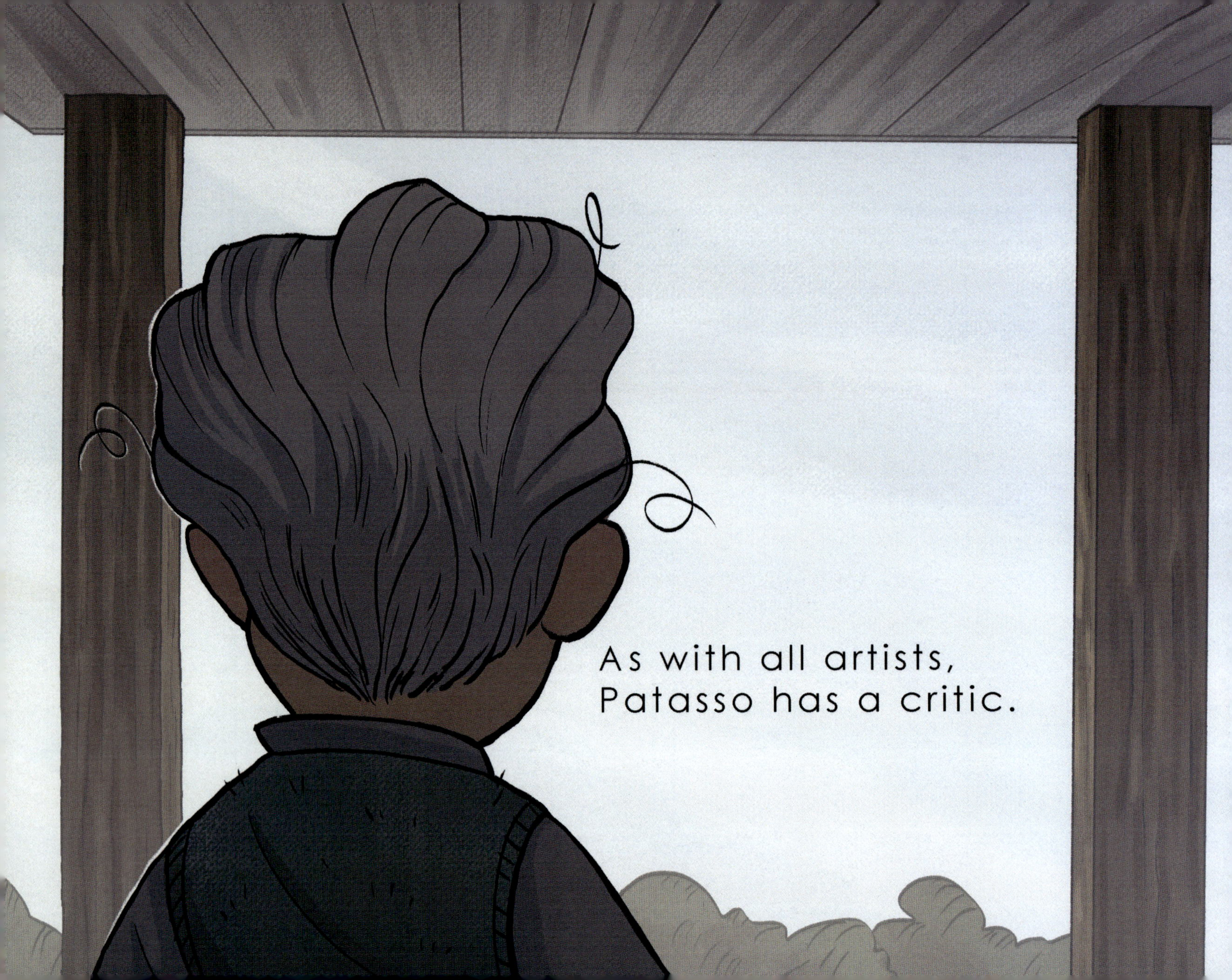
As with all artists,
Patasso has a critic.

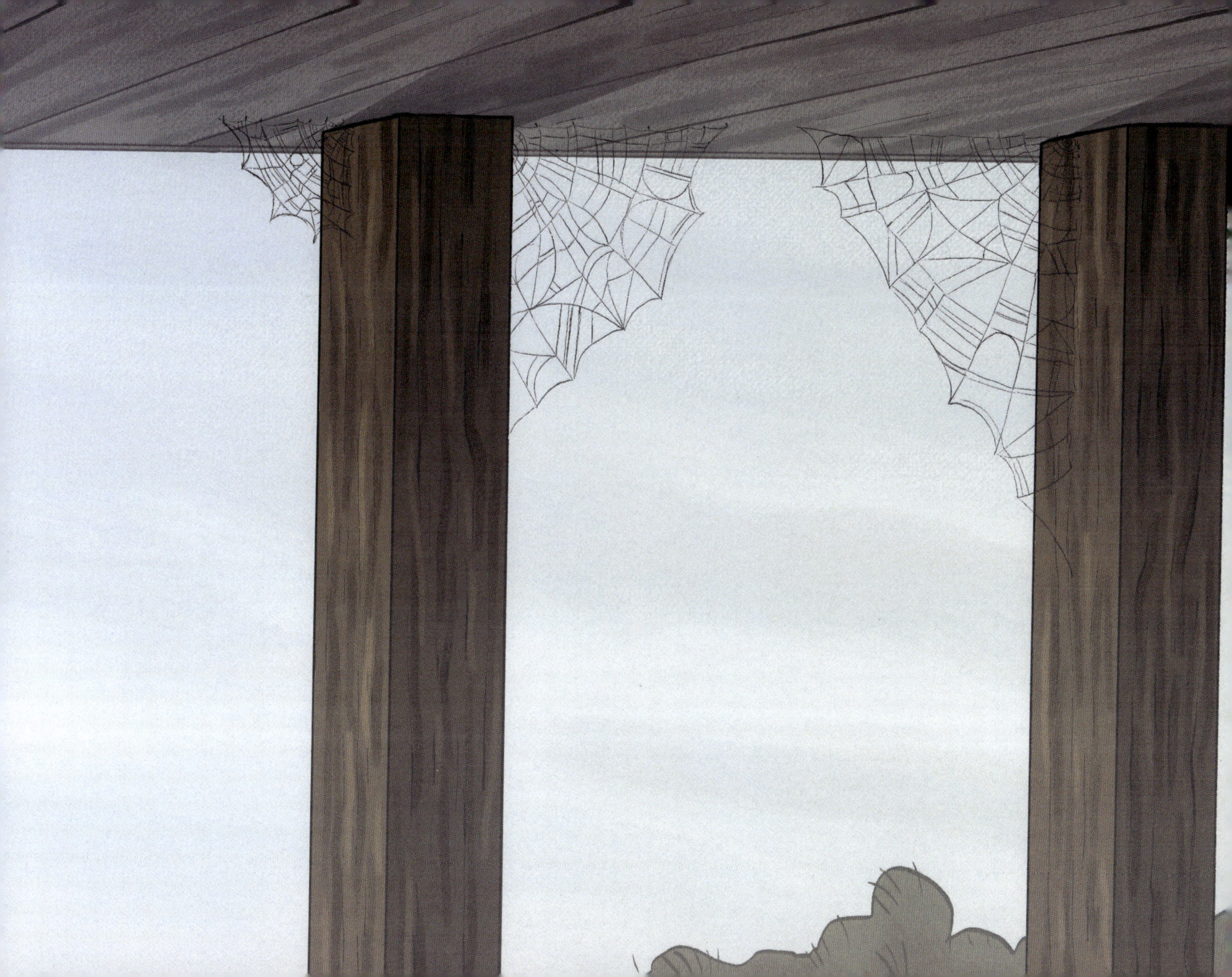

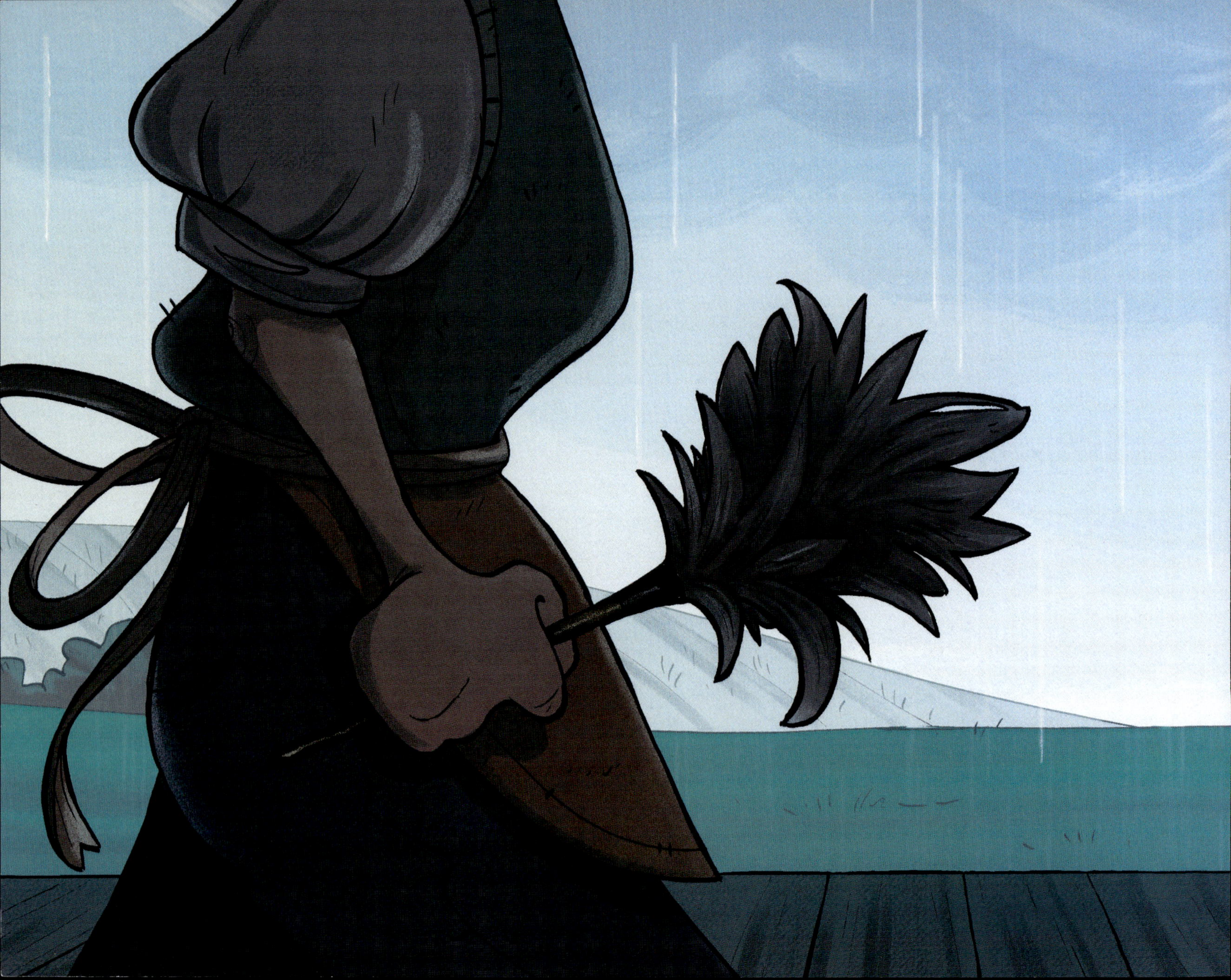

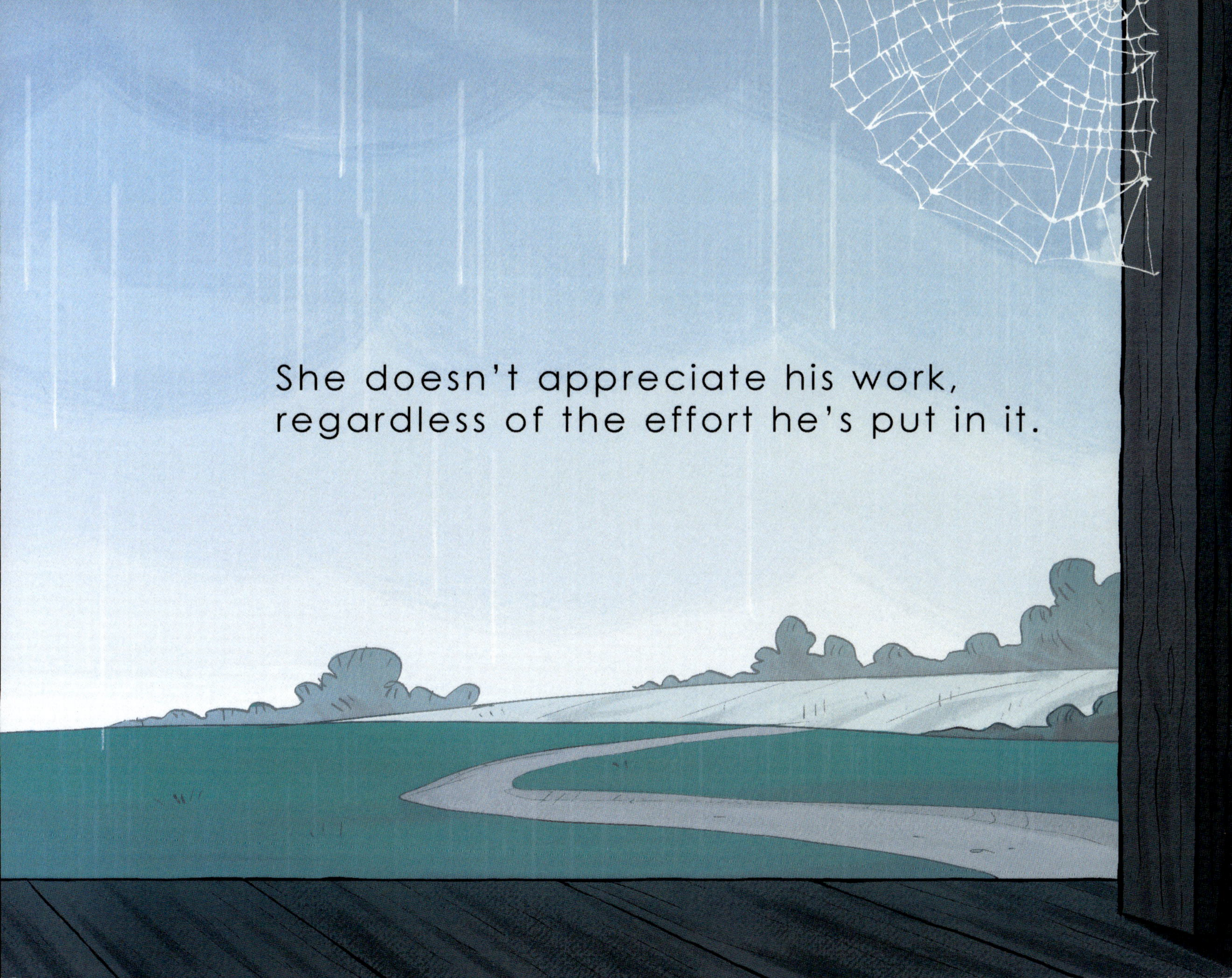

She doesn't appreciate his work,
regardless of the effort he's put in it.

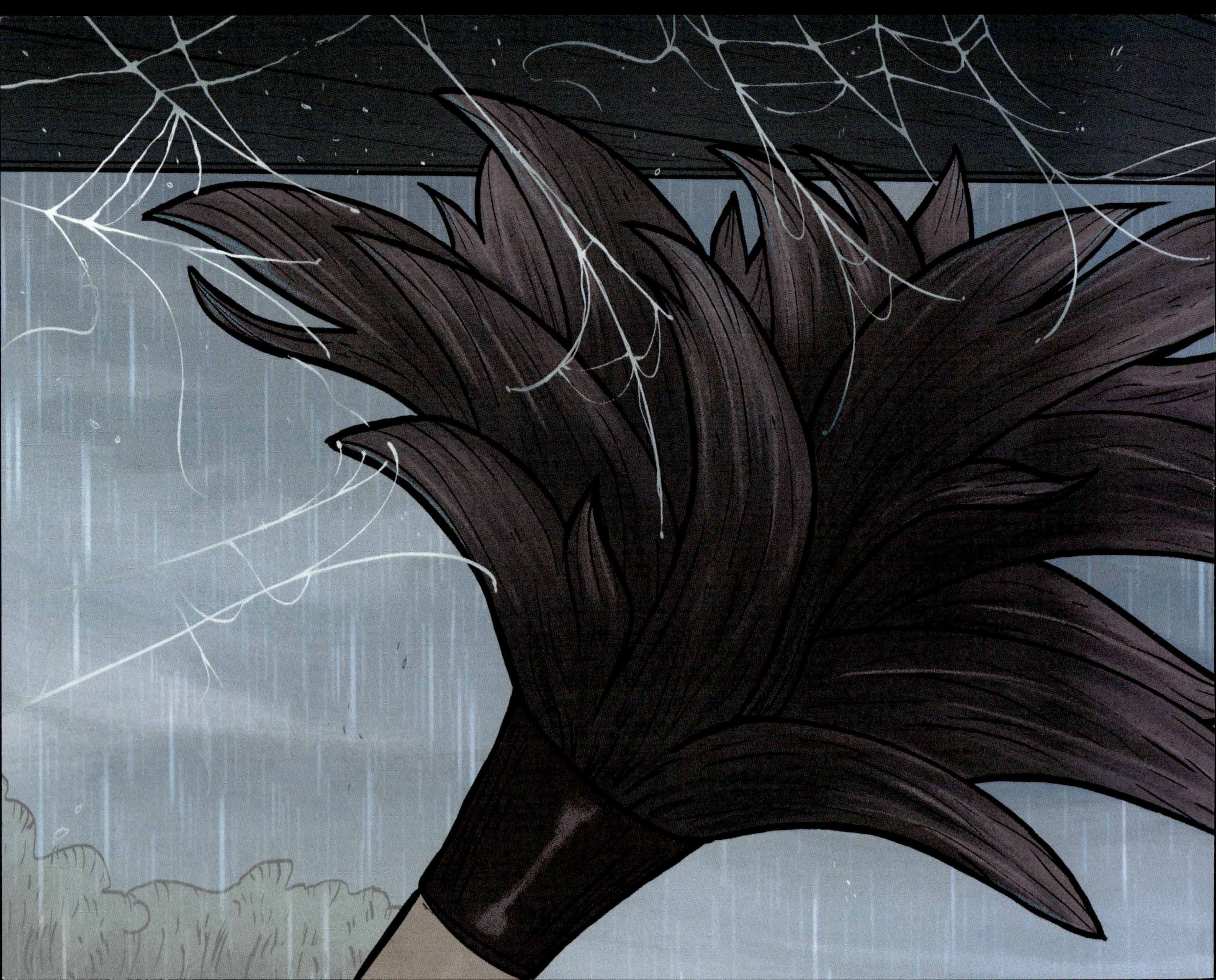

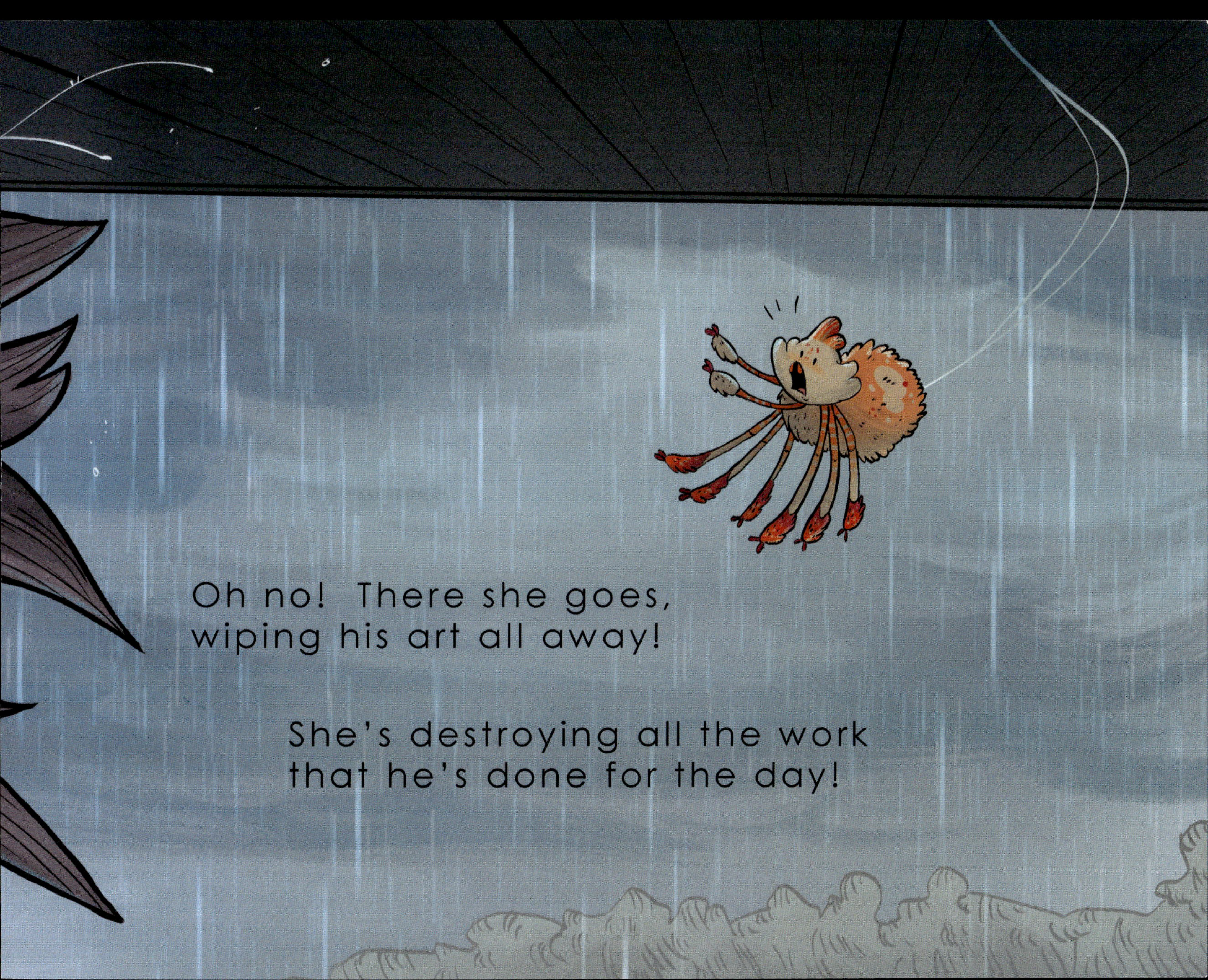

Oh no! There she goes,
wiping his art all away!

She's destroying all the work
that he's done for the day!

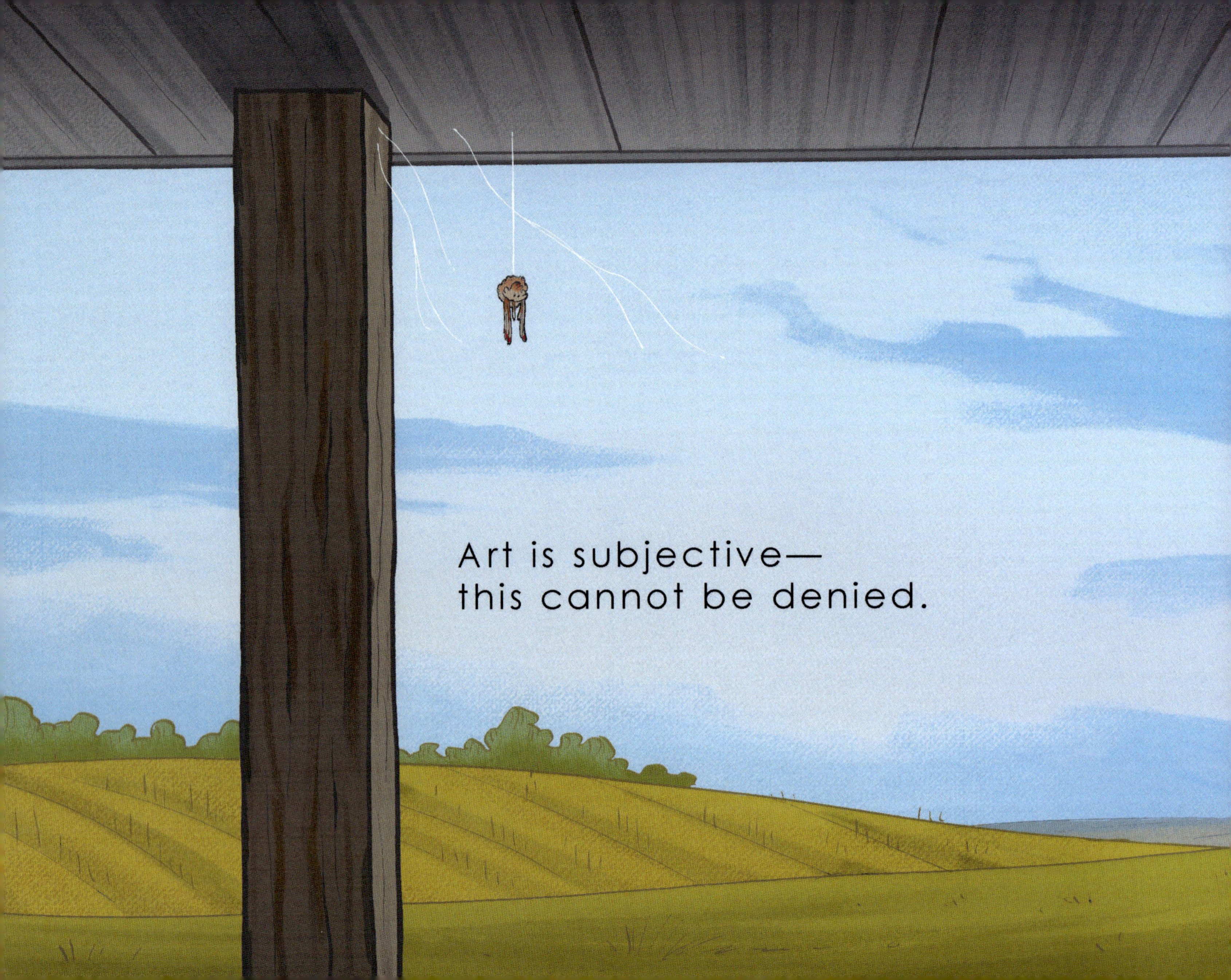

Art is subjective—
this cannot be denied.

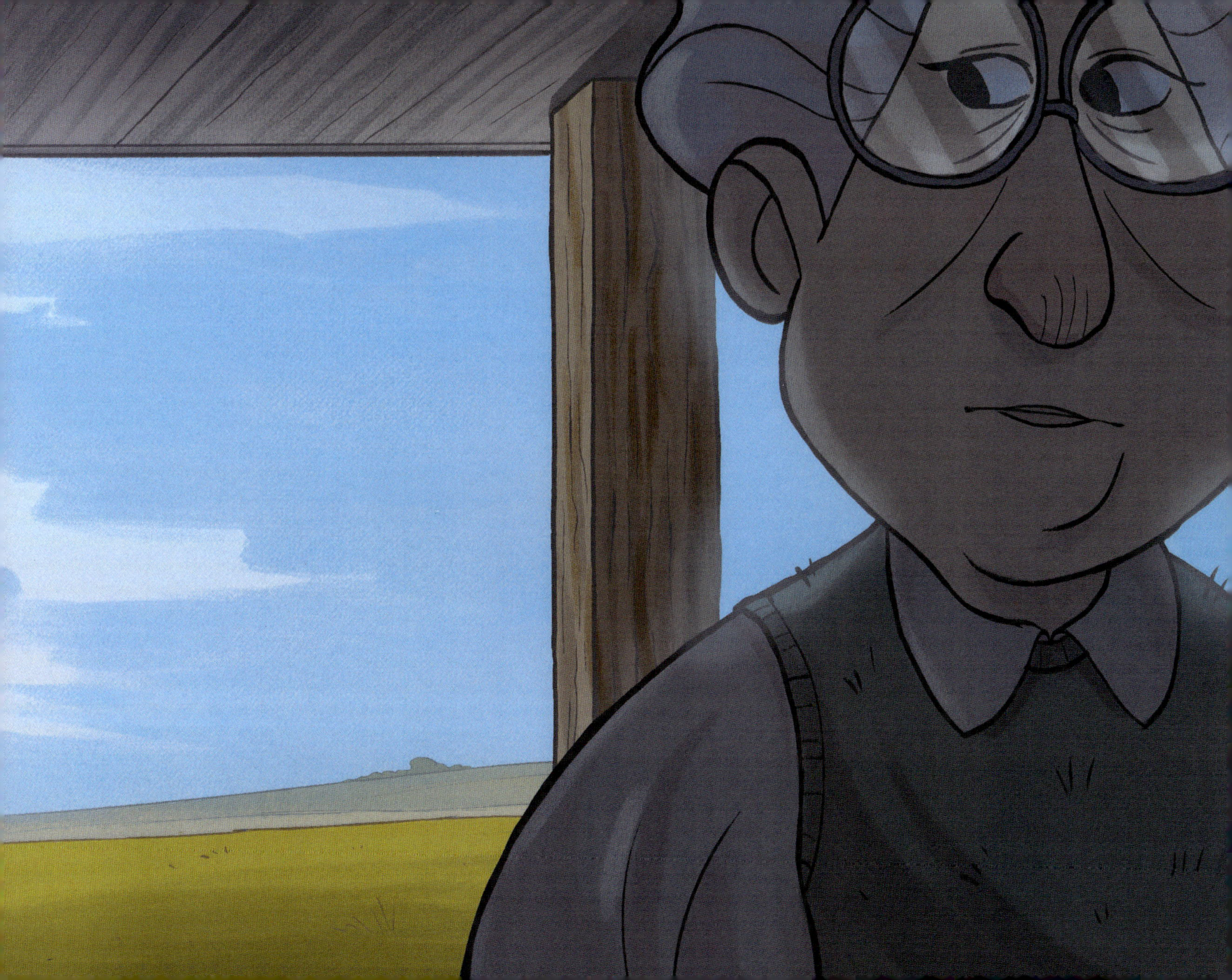

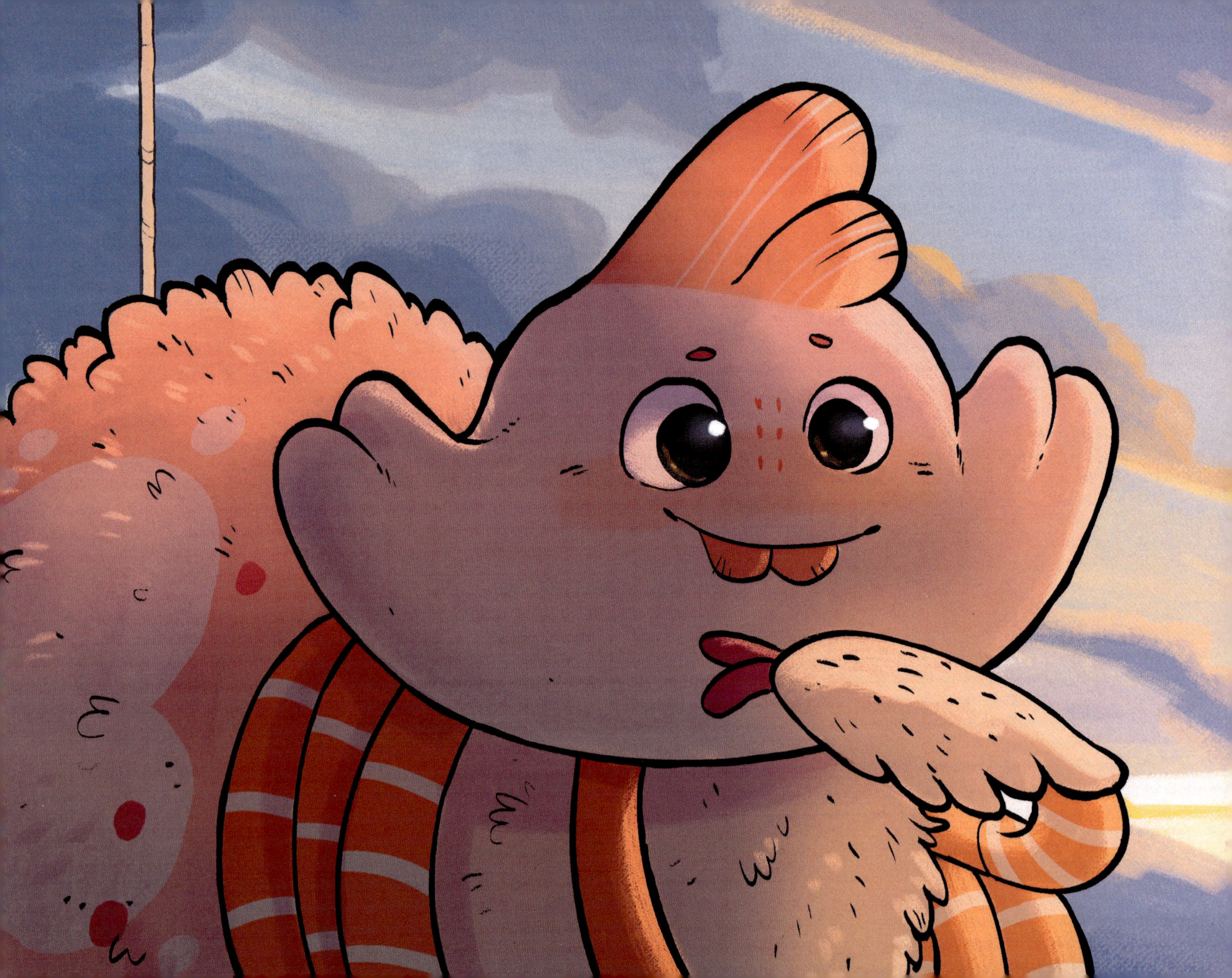

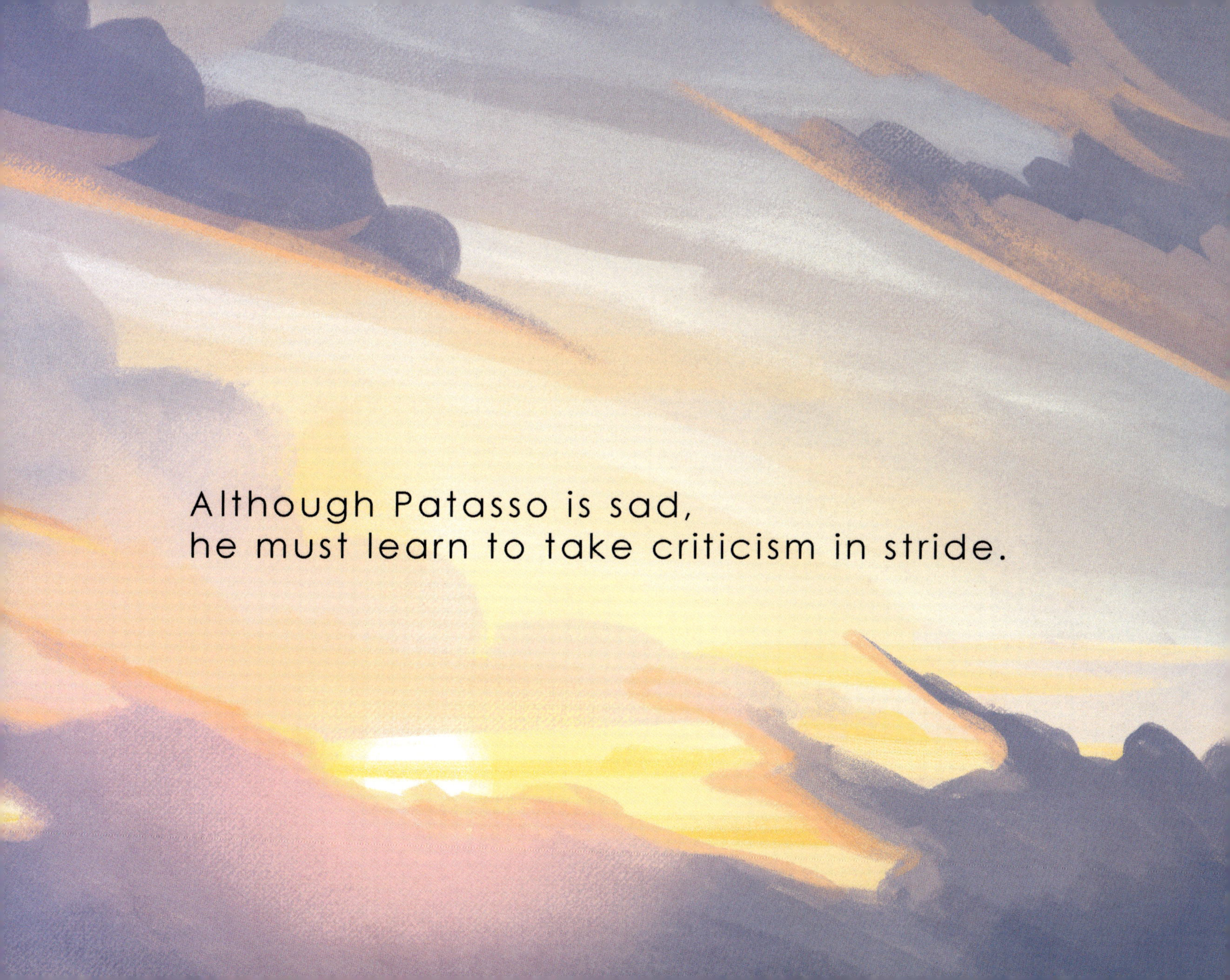
Although Patasso is sad,
he must learn to take criticism in stride.

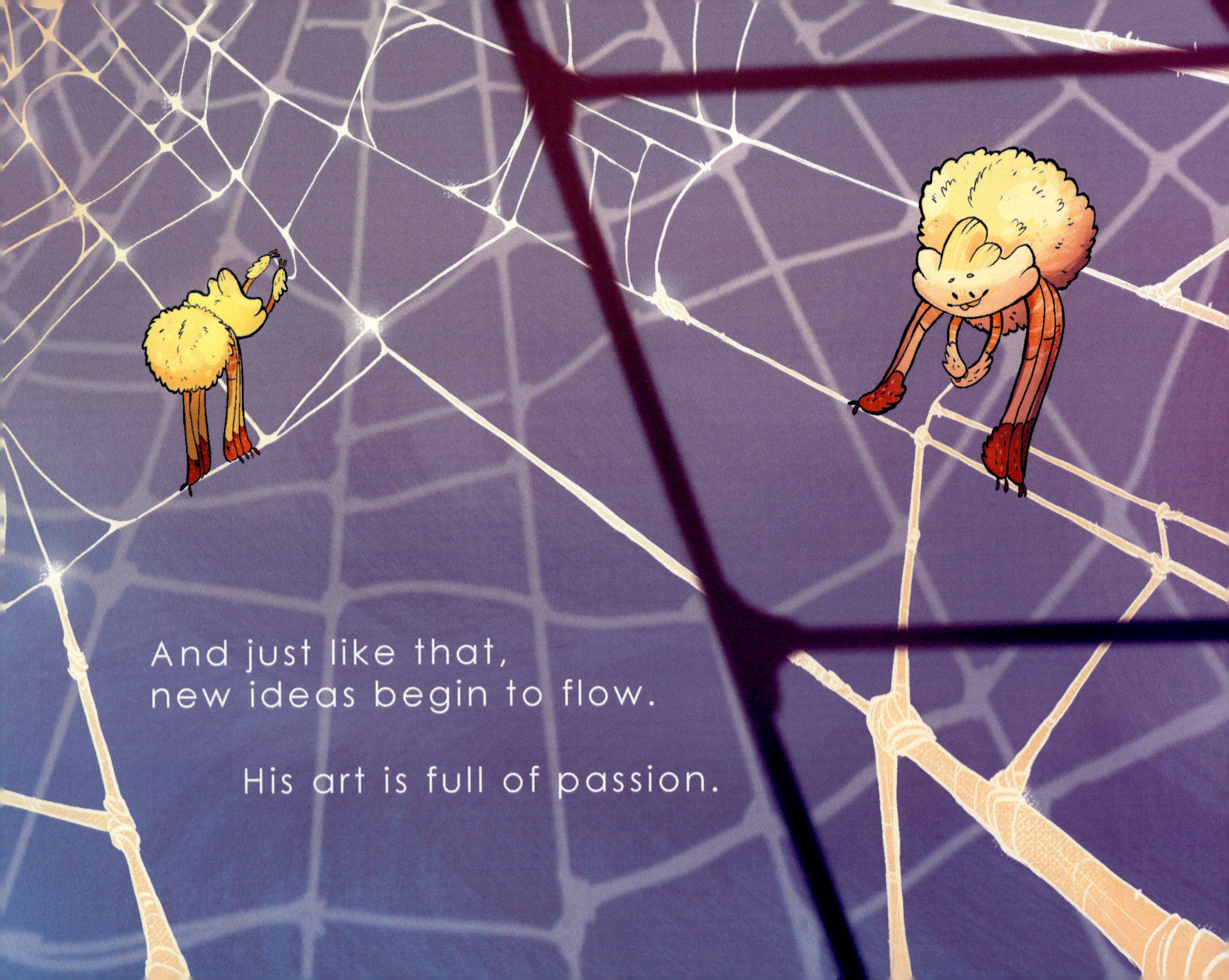
And just like that,
new ideas begin to flow.

His art is full of passion.

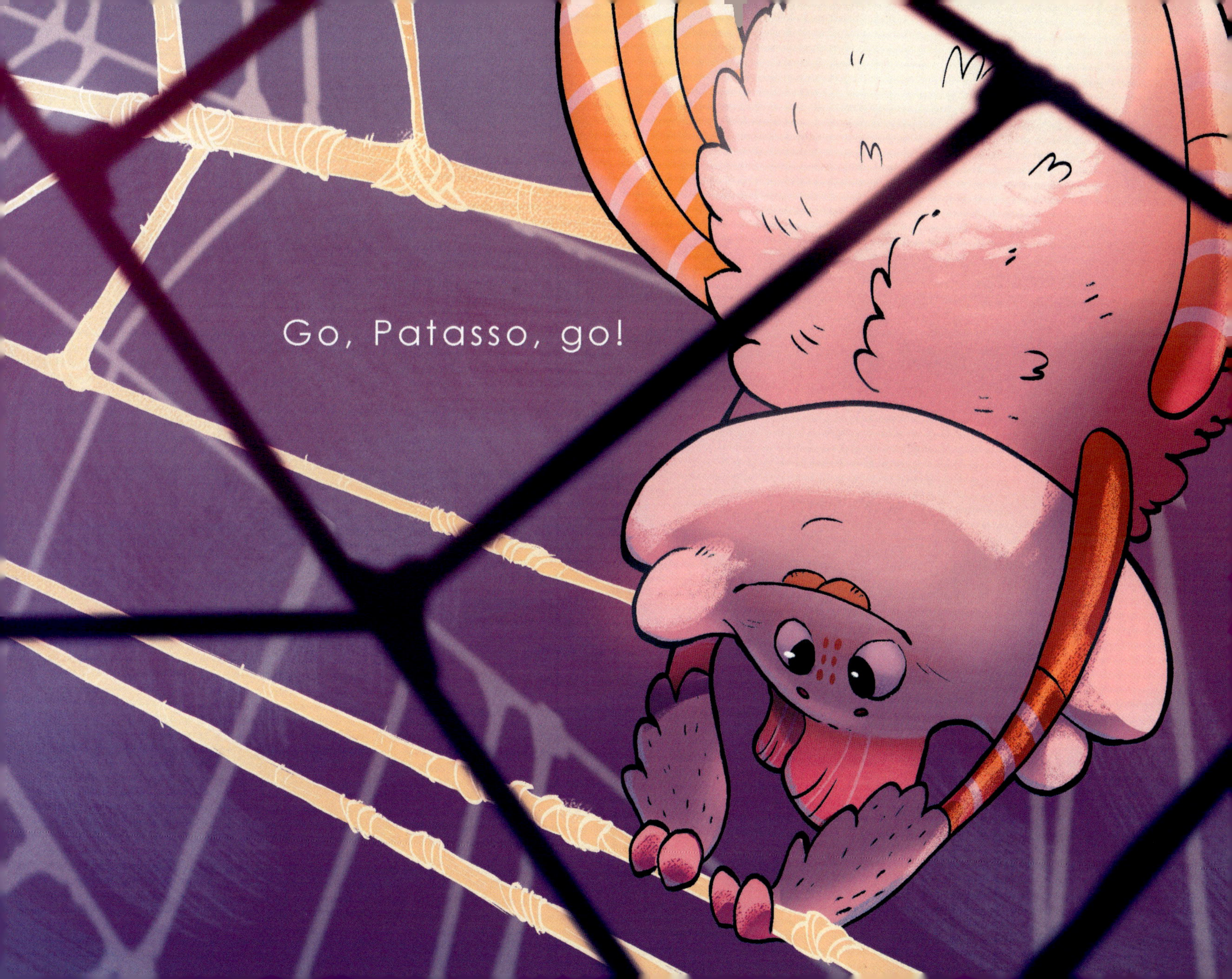
Go, Patasso, go!

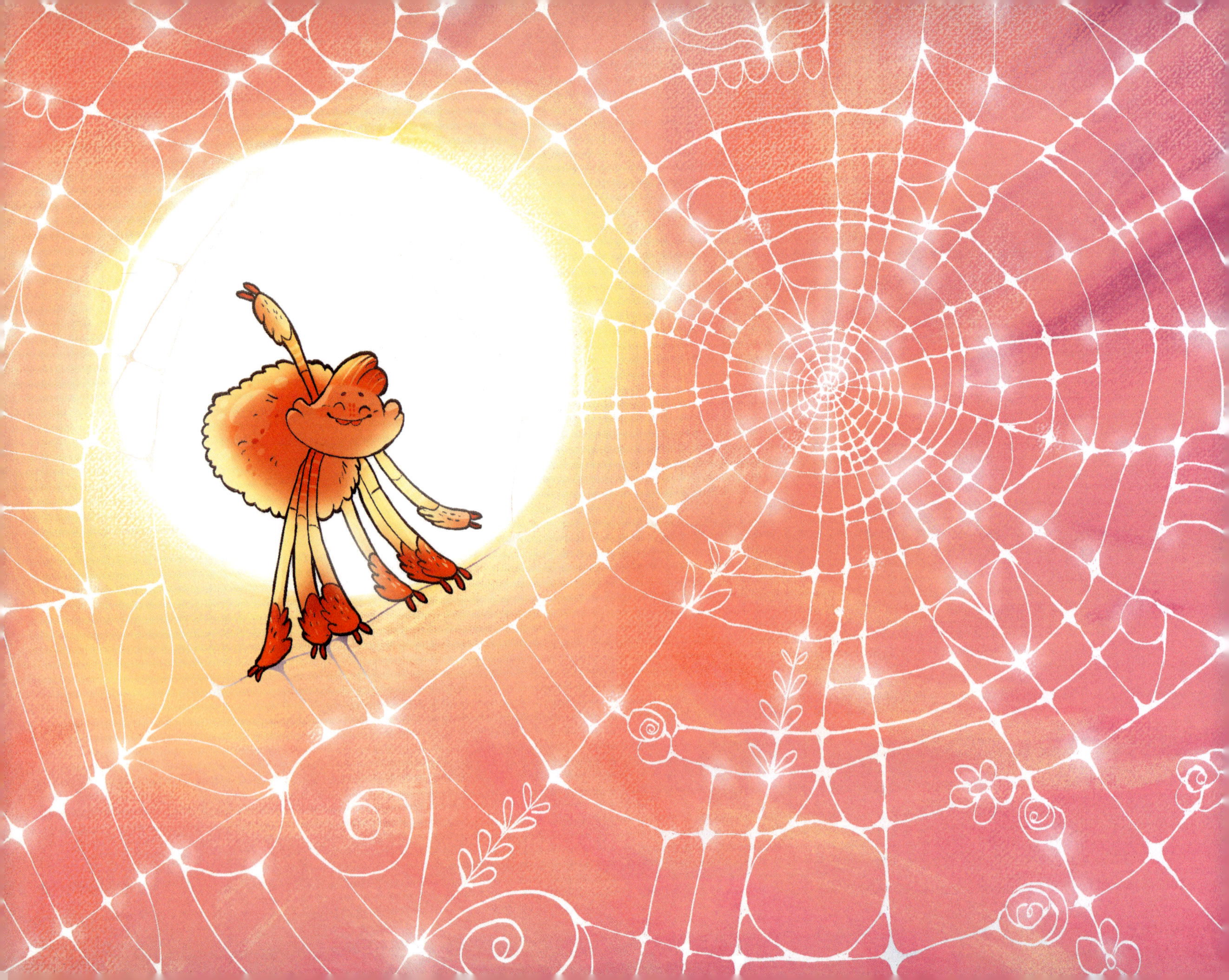

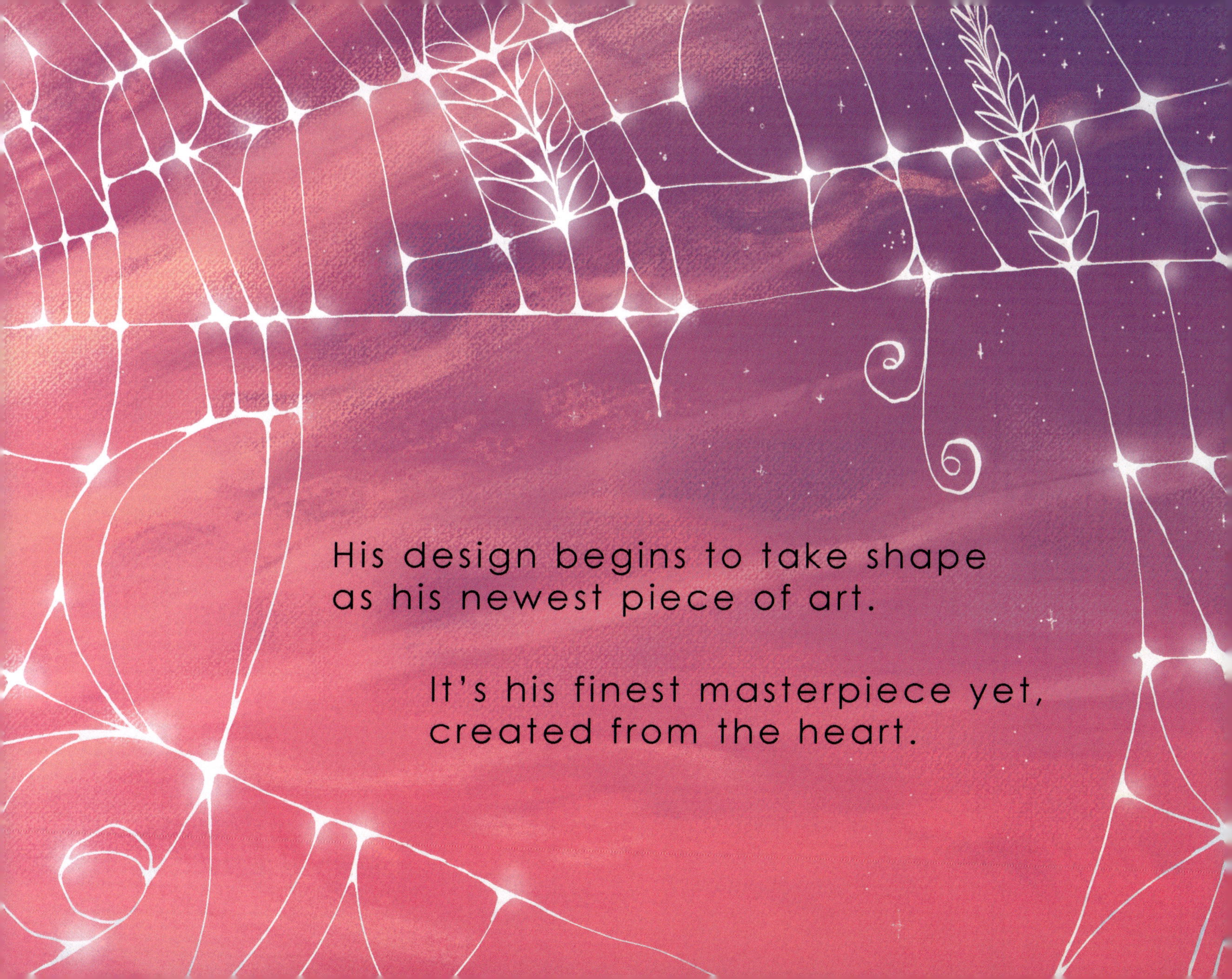

His design begins to take shape
as his newest piece of art.

It's his finest masterpiece yet,
created from the heart.

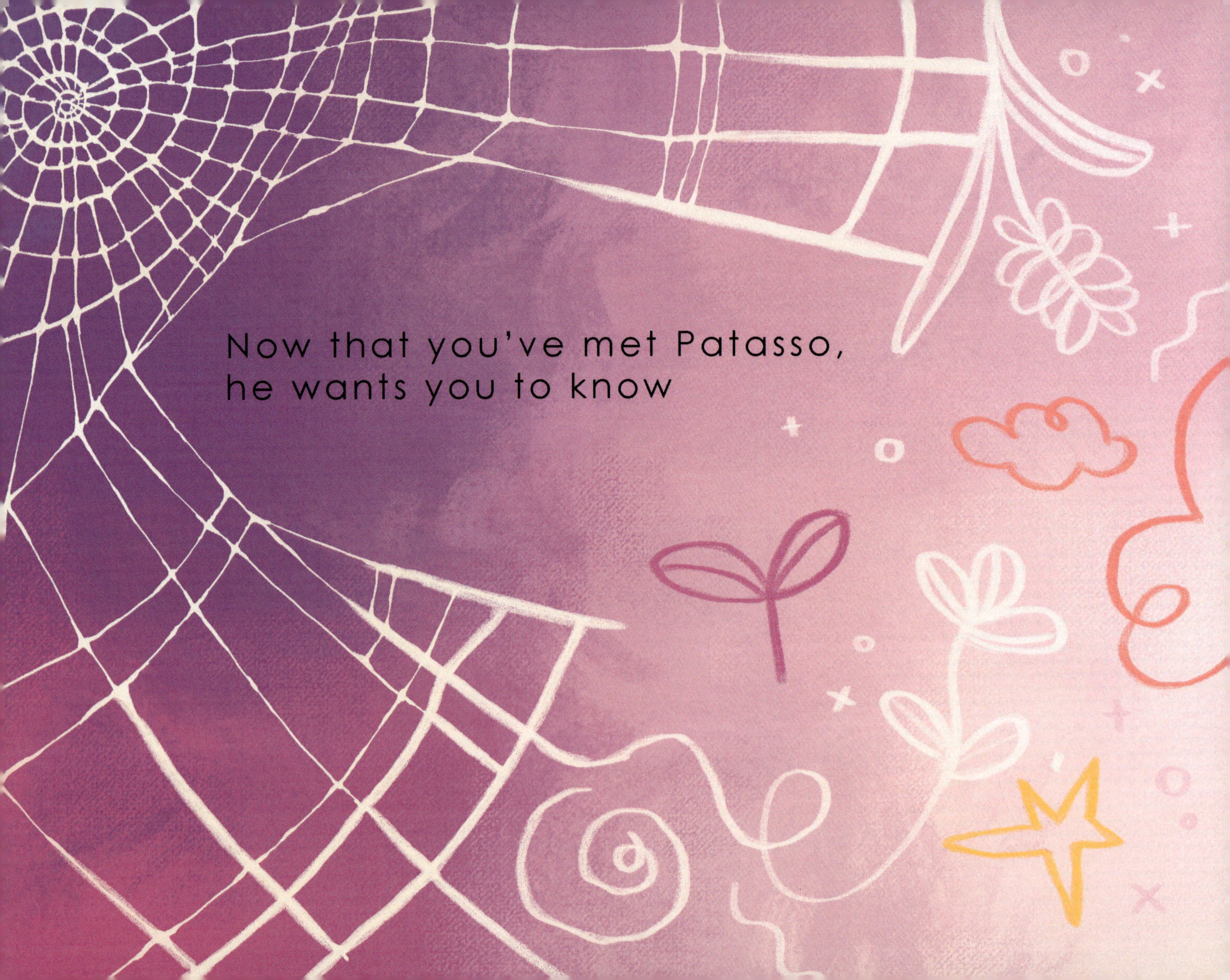

Now that you've met Patasso,
he wants you to know

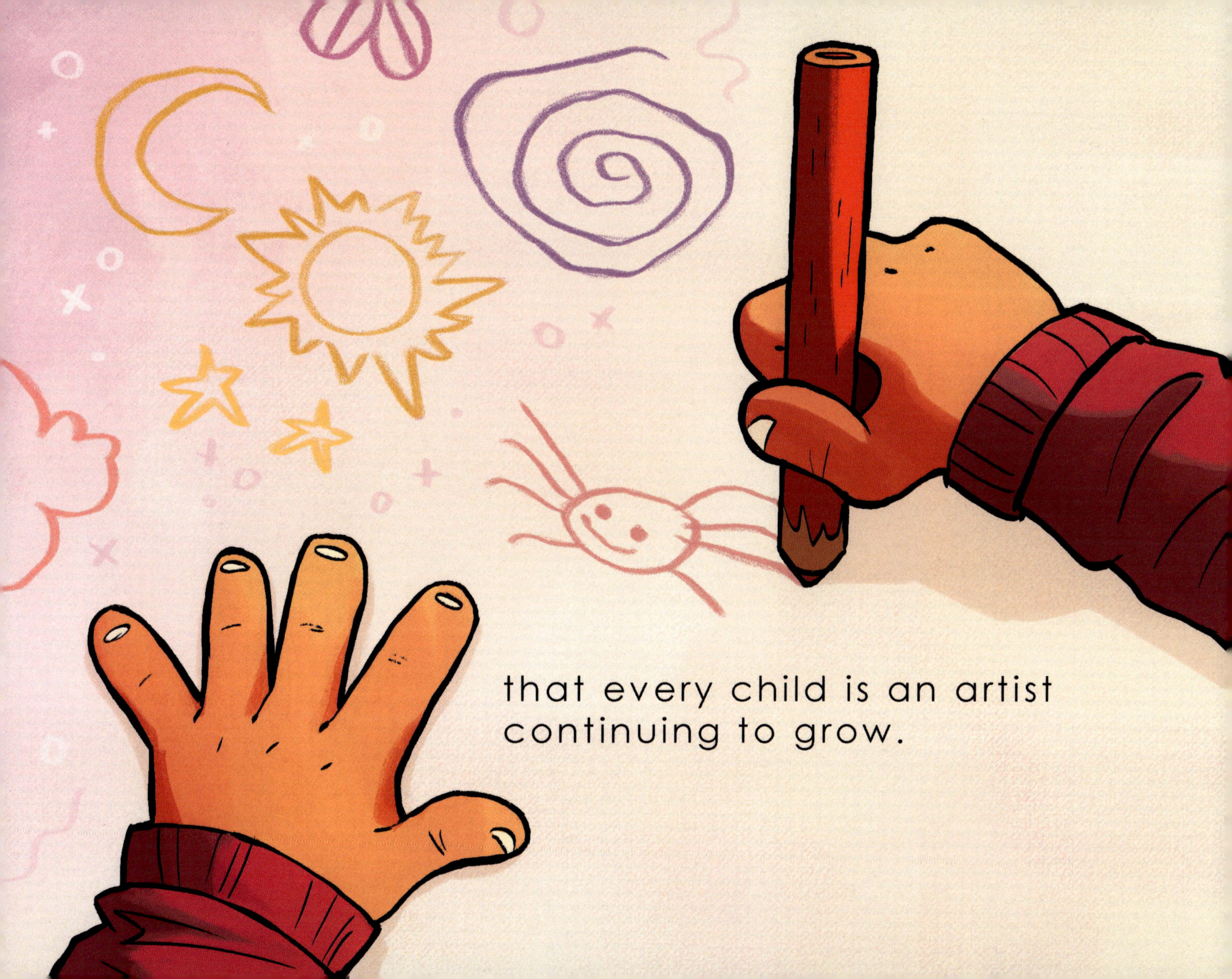

that every child is an artist
continuing to grow.

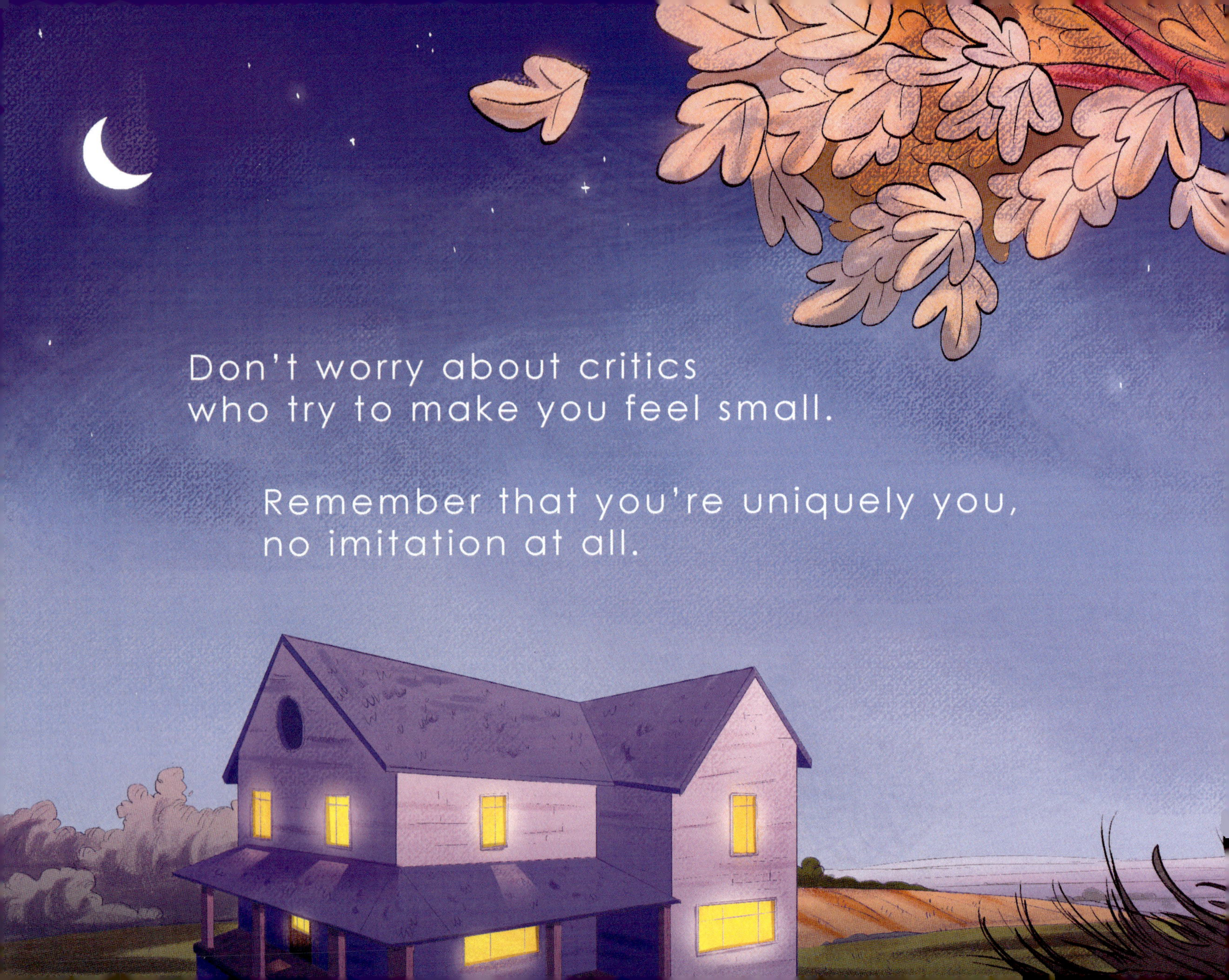
Don't worry about critics
who try to make you feel small.

Remember that you're uniquely you,
no imitation at all.

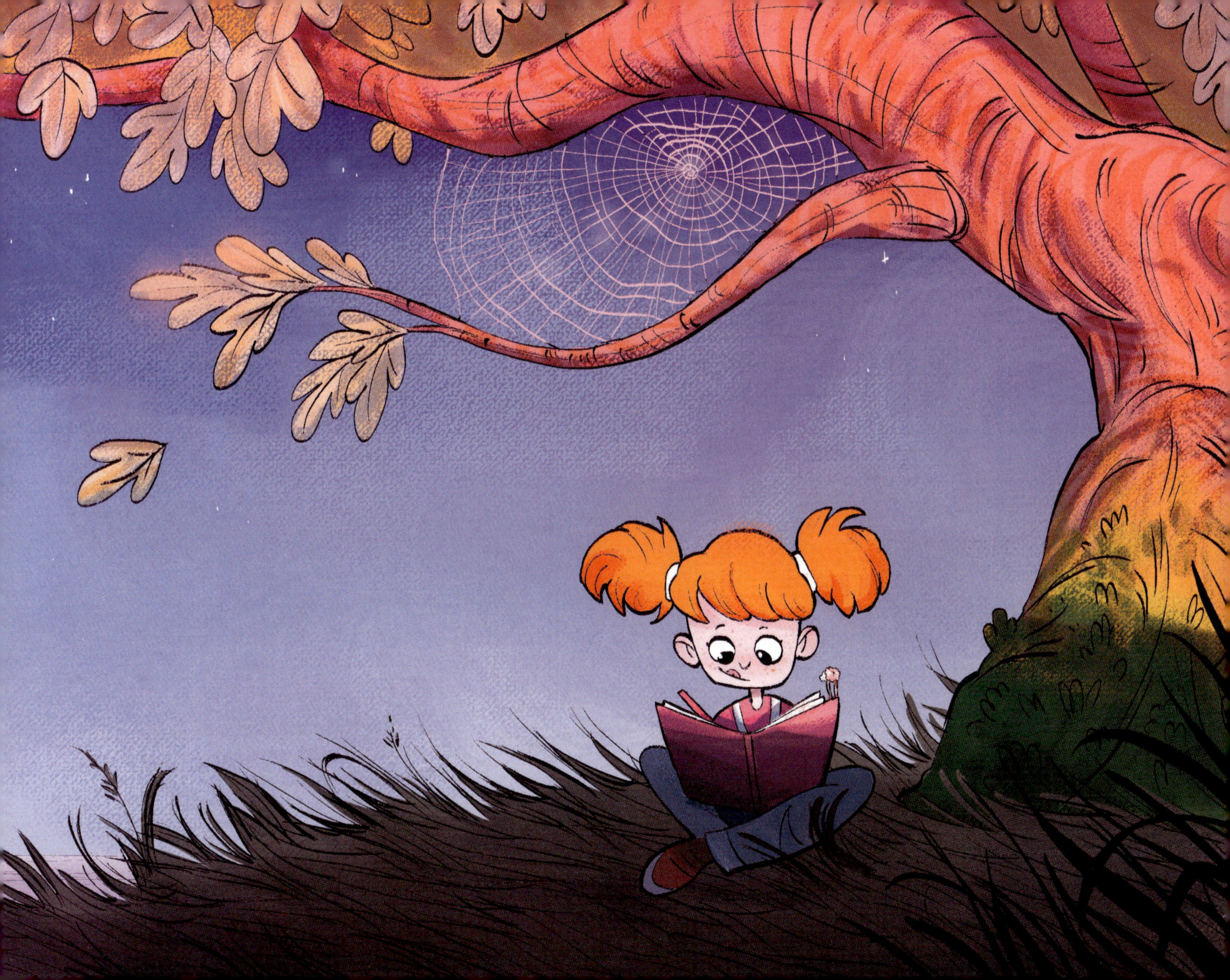

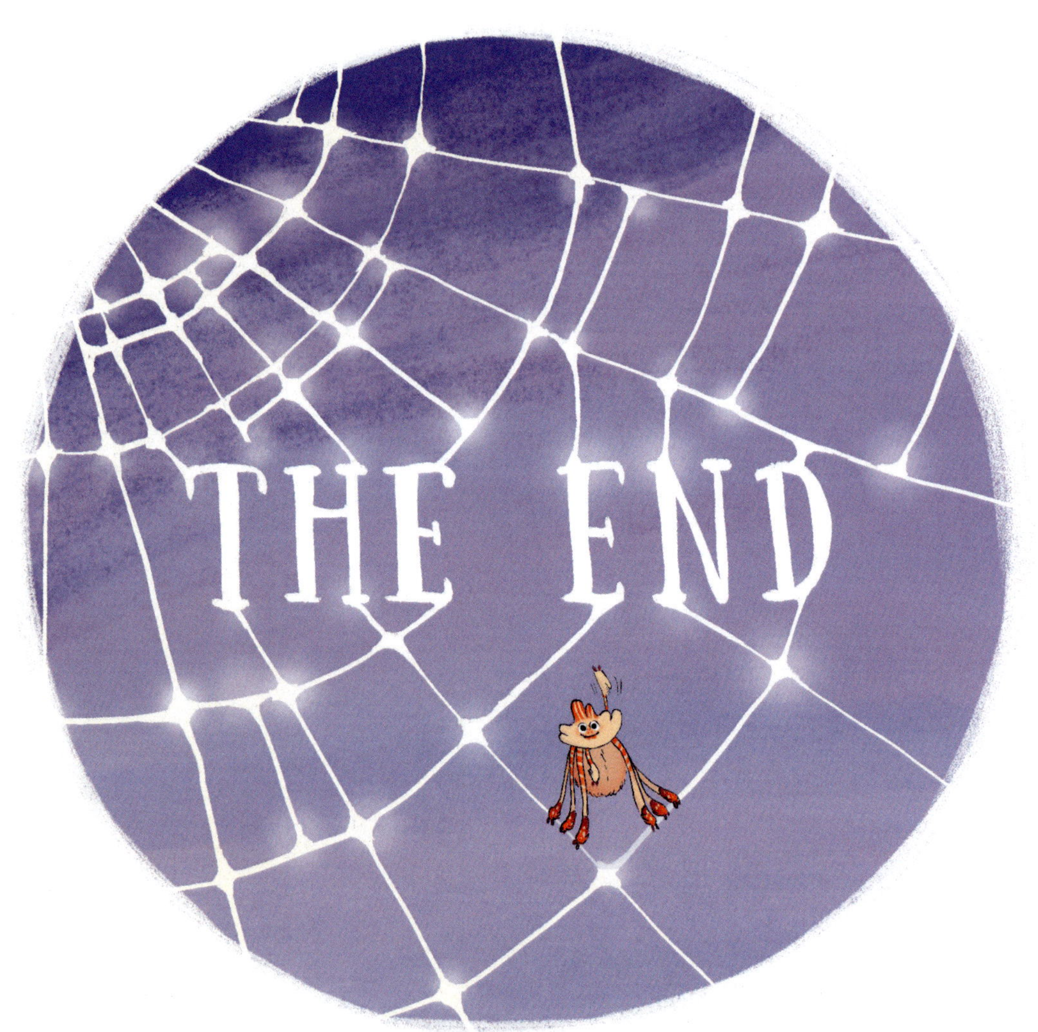

THE END

Tracy Bayley

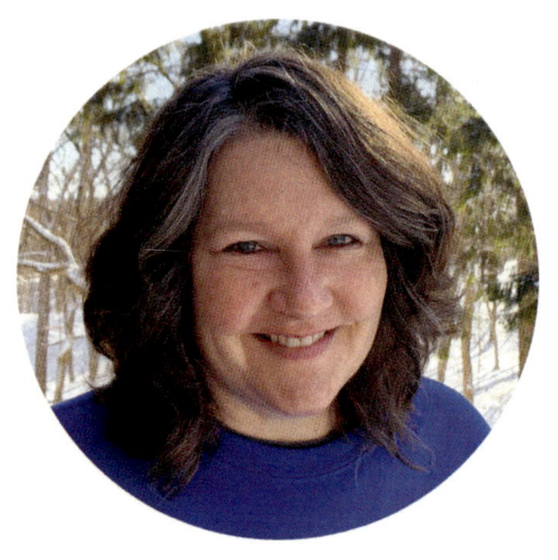

Tracy's favorite words are "What if..." due to her inquisitive nature.

After receiving her bachelor's degree in graphic design, Tracy launched a lengthy career as a retail marketing executive. Ready to start a new adventure as a storyteller, she finished writing Patasso and is reviving characters from stories she brought to life for her daughters when they were young.

Julia Elaine

One part artist, one part storyteller,
a dash of creativity, a pinch of outgoing,
and a heaping helpful of horse-loving
is the recipe for a Julia Elaine!

A summa cum laude graduate from the
Milwaukee Institute of Art & Design, she is
most often spotted drawing up stories of her
own creation or astride her trusty steed -
a quarter horse named Valentine.

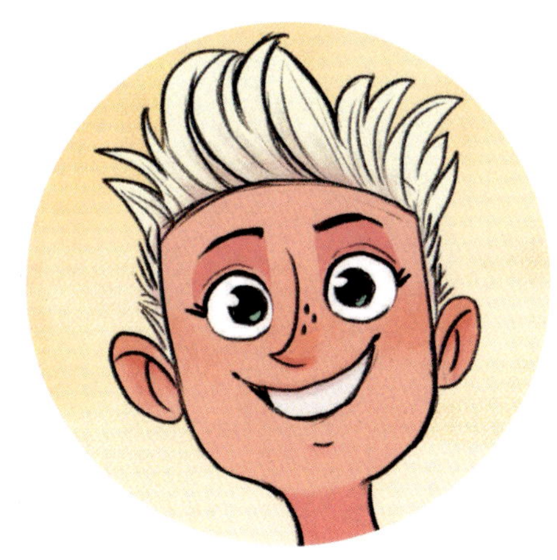

juliaelaine.wixsite.com   juliaelaine.illus@gmail.com

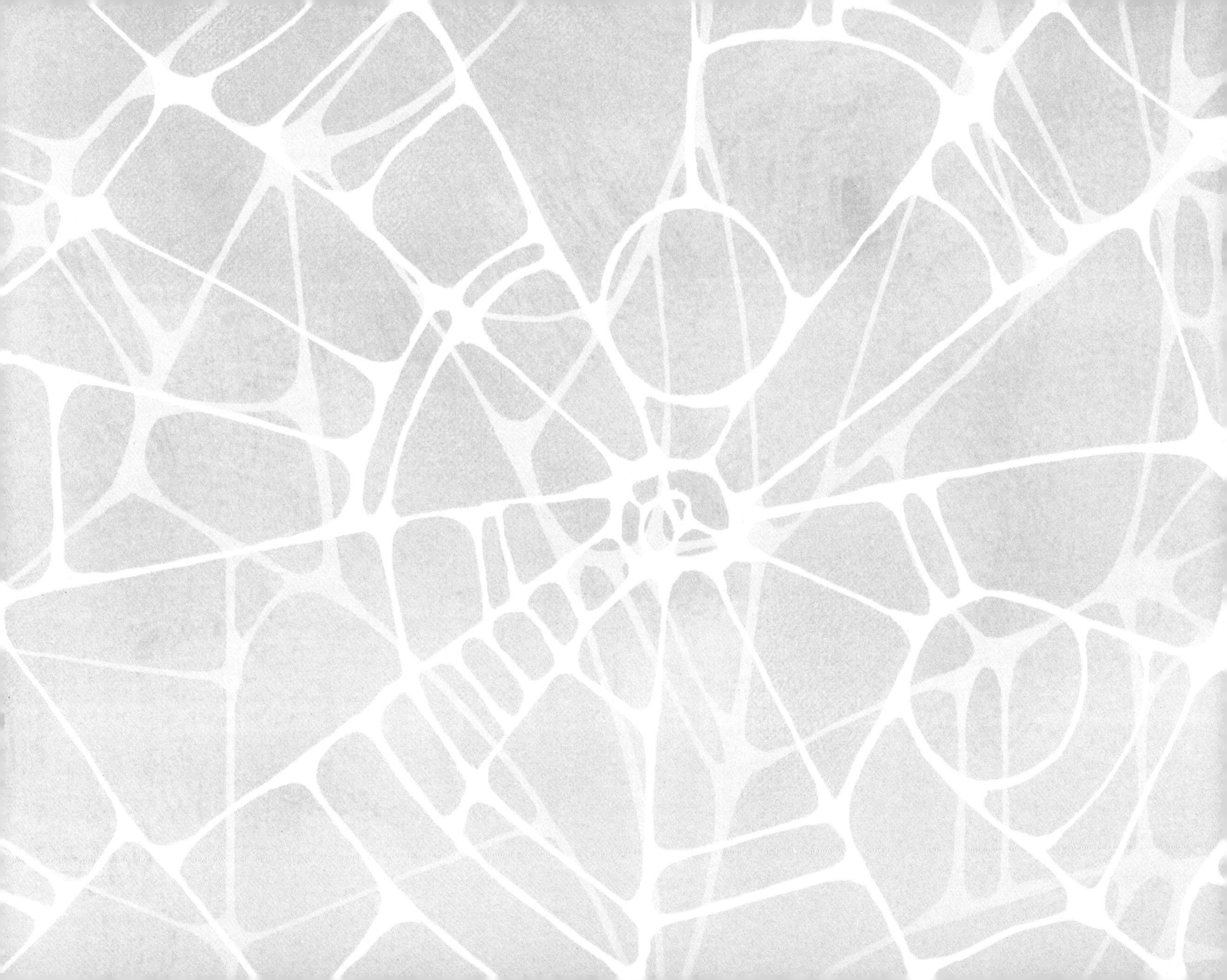